ALONG THE RIVER

An Anthology of Voices from the

Río Grande Valley

Edited by

David Bowles

VAO Publishing
A division of *Valley Artistic Outreach*
4717 N FM 493
Donna, TX 78537
www.publishing.valartout.org

ISBN: 978-0615480664

First printed edition: May 2011

CONTENTS

CONTRIBUTOR BIOGRAPHIES

FOREWARD

When a small group of like-minded local artists founded Valley Artistic Outreach in 2010, they were driven by a shared vision of the need to promote art across south Texas. VAO's principal mission would be to go into communities throughout the Río Grande Valley and provide art workshops to kids who—because of their socio-economic status or because their schools had abandoned the arts to focus on state testing—had no access to the sorts of horizon-expanding activities that tend to put more affluent students at a distinct advantage.

But VAO is also about ensuring that adults have a venue for their artistic expression. It is essential, in our view, that human beings have a creative outlet for their dreams, emotions, ideas. A life without art is somehow poorer, we feel, and as a result, we have dedicated ourselves to providing opportunities for self-expression.

This twin mission has resulted in our collaboration with entities such as Douglas Clark Studio and the Texas A & M Colonias Program to carry out our many arts workshops and to host the multiple art exhibits and performances that we have arranged.

The present volume represents both a continuation of the work we did during our first year and our exploration of a new area of the arts that we had not to this point focused on: the language and literature of this region, its peculiar rhythms and accents, the rich culture that it so eloquently encodes.

The contributors to *Along the River* range from established authors to emerging voices, from teachers to students, from businesswomen to retirees and everything in between. Like our Valley, it is a beautiful patchwork of cultures and ethnicities, and we at VAO hope that it will be the first of many volumes that drape this worthy quilt before the eyes of the world.

In a time in which federal and state funding for the arts is being slashed even further, this collection will be a boon to artists and children. With the proceeds from the sale of *Along the River*, VAO will continue its dual mission, helping to nourish the seed that the arts can plant in the heart of every member of our community.

By purchasing the book you hold in your hands, you have become a partner in that very worthy endeavor, and we thank you.

David Bowles
April 25, 2011

PROSE

SELECTIONS

THE TIME ABOUT THE DOG

After the party, Celestino drove to the Texas Bar in town. It was a small place, with a red neon beer sign in the window. When he walked in, a little bell above the door tinkled a welcome. It had been a long time since he had allowed himself this luxury. There was a bar, and stools, but he took a booth and Ramiro came over to take his drink. Tino asked for a Jax and Ramiro went away and came back with a can of beer and a glass. He opened the can and set both in front of Tino. Then he left.

Tino looked at the open can and glass. What could they bring him but misery? No, not misery. Forgetting. They could bring him forgetting the story he'd told at the party tonight, the memory that was fresh in his mind as if he was a boy again and it had been yesterday.

He filled the glass. His hands were steady as he did. How long could he keep up this act? He wondered. Did it matter? No. He decided it didn't. And when he realized it, he also saw he had emptied the glass. How long had that taken? How long had he nursed the beer? What was time anyway? He lifted the empty glass and Ramiro was there with another can of Jax.

"Want me to pour it?" Ramiro asked.

"No." Tino said. "I'll do it."

Ramiro left, and Tino poured. It went on that way for a long while, or a short while. When Ramiro returned for the last time, he didn't have a can of Jax with him.

"It's done," Ramiro told him. "Let me have your keys. I'll drive you home."

"You can have my truck, Ramiro. I'm giving it to you."

Ramiro looked around the bar. "Say that when there are witnesses, *cabrón,"* he said. "Come on. Let's go."

"No," Tino said. "Take the keys. I want to walk."

"You're joking. Come on. I'll drive you."

"I'm not joking. I want to walk. I'm walking. You keep the truck."

Ramiro seemed to consider it a while. "Go ahead. Walk. It's one of the nicest nights we've had in a long time. I'll bring your truck to your house tomorrow."

"Thank you, Ramiro."

He exited the bar then, walking proudly if slowly into the empty street. He patted the side of his truck as if wishing it well. He went on then, into the night of forgetting, past the places where streetlights still stood, into the darkness.

The moon lit the earth. The wind embraced him, then rushed past him, chasing memory away. Where was he? Where was he going? It pleased him that he couldn't remember. There was only the road.

He saw its form before he identified it, and its eyes shining like opals in the moonlight. His mind registered what it had seen, connected it with the word *coyote*, then just as quickly the word eluded him again.

It was watching him, he was sure. Maybe it was rabid or at, the very least, famished, and would go for his throat when it was close enough to leap. But as he drew nearer, he saw it wasn't a coyote at all but a dog of mixed breeds, a ranch mutt. Taller than most ranch mutts, perhaps, but dusty and dirty as any he had seen, with a name like Bullet or Jumper or Perro Chingado. Now that he was closer, he could also see that there was a kindness behind those opal eyes, luminous and warm, and Tino felt he had found something he had been searching for a long time.

The dog walked beside him then, a step or two ahead, leading Tino across the ranch land into the moonlight. He would follow him anywhere. They crossed pastures and brush, thick in places, but they passed unscathed by mesquite branches or the loping tear-shaped leaves of *nopales*.

He had walked a long time, he was sure, but he wasn't tired. He felt alive. Young. A boy.

There was music. God only knew where it came from, but he heard it, and was sure the dog heard it, too. Then it was gone. But he had heard it, though he could not think of words to describe it except to say that it was beautiful.

When he saw his house, Tino began to cry. It was a sad, silent weeping, and he tasted the salt and sweat of his tears as they fell. *I am drunk, goddamnit, and there is no way I could have walked home from town.*

As he walked and wept, he looked down and patted the dog's head. There was a word for this. It was forming behind his eyes, forming and disintegrating, the syllables refusing to come. Then it was there—*cadejo*. It was a story he'd heard a friend of his grandfather's tell. A *cadejo* is a dog that sees drunks safely home. The word had made him chuckle as a boy because it sounded like *pendejo*. But here it was again, not a story, but his life. He had stumbled across a myth in his drunkenness. He had lived a legend. He wished he had a mirror to see himself, perhaps he had turned into paper, printed pages of a book, or maybe just words stacked on top of each other, one sliding over the other in the fury of the telling, or maybe he was just the sound of the words, the calming echo of the story. The tears really came now, and the dog looked up at him with understanding, uncanny and real in his eyes.

"I don't ever want to tell anyone this story," he told the dog. "I thank you for what you did, but I can't tell it. I can't tell another story."

The dog eyed him, his tongue hanging low and angled over his lower teeth.

"Wait here," he said as they came to the door. "I'm going to get you some meat."

He went to the refrigerator, took out the steak, unwrapped it from the butcher paper and set it on the doorstep. He looked around, whistled, but the *cadejo* was gone. He sat on the stoop and waited but the dog never returned.

In the morning, his wife found him on the doorstep. She didn't say anything, just made the coffee to have it ready for him when he awoke. She would make him *chorizo con huevo* and corn tortillas. Then she would ask him what the hell he did with the truck.

Álvaro Rodríguez

LORD TLACUACHE BRINGS FIRE TO MAN

Lord Tlacuache, the Great Opossum, ruled this land in ages past, when animals still spoke and mankind had not yet usurped the earth. He was a kindly king who governed by virtue of his clever mind, and nothing pleased him more than to see his subjects happy.

Tlacuache, in fact, once used his nimble hands to dig deep into a mature maguey plant and draw forth the delicious sap waiting within. Storing this *aguamiel* in gourds, he discovered fermentation, and the joy-bringing drink we call *pulque* was invented. Soon animals up and down his vast kingdom were producing the beverage, and in celebration Lord Tlacuache went on a binge, stumbling from cantina to cantina, leaving behind a meandering set of trails that eventually became the rivers of Mexico, including this, our Río Bravo.

Most creatures were content with the quiet ebb and flow of the world, safe and at ease within Lord Tlacuache's broad demesne.

Except for men.

It was not enough that food aplenty was within Man's grasp: he wanted more.

It was not enough that prey surrendered themselves to Man according to the natural order: Man wanted to cook his prey.

Man had discovered fire when lightning stuck and set a tree or two alight, but he was clumsy and greedy and stupid and could not keep the flame alive.

In vain Man rushed after the sun as it plunged each evening past the edge of the earth into Mictlán, the vast and daunting underworld. He hoped to catch a falling ray of heat to take back to his cave.

But all Man's foolish plans came to naught, so in desperation he came before Lord Tlacuache.

"We are cold and our food is raw. Please help us, clever and revered opossum!"

"What happened to the fire you got from that burning tree?" Tlacuache asked.

"We fell asleep after drinking pulque and let the coals die out. Now we shiver and our stomachs ache."

Tlacuache looked upon mankind and was moved to pity. He did not want a single one of his subjects to suffer or be unhappy. But obtaining fire was a terrifying task. He would be putting his very life at risk. Still, his heart yearned to bring Man joy, so he agreed.

"I will bring you fire, but you must take better care of it this time."

Man bent his head in shamed reverence and swore to keep the flame alive.

Tlacuache first gathered his gourds of pulque and then set off toward the West, following the sun as it slipped down the sky. At the edge of the world, the brave lord of this land slipped quietly down the path the sun's passing had left, using his tail and nimble hands to navigate the straitest patches, playing dead whenever a skeletal guardian of Mictlán happened to come along.

Soon he nearly caught up with the sun, but the flaming disk was accompanied by Xolotl, the massive, toothy hound of hell. Tlacuache had no desire to confront that growling psychopomp, so he stayed out of sight, following the pair as they made their way deeper into the bowels of Mictlán.

Finally the sun reached the hearth of the fire god, Xiuhtecuhtli, and Xolotl left to guide more souls to their final abode. The fire god began to tend to the needs of the sun, feeding its heat with wood and coal, giving it some needed rest.

As if he had been invited, Tlacuache scampered up to Xiuhtecuhtli and gave a little bow. "My Lord," he intoned.

The fire god, who was also the patron of kings and brave warriors, looked surprised to see the opossum, but recognized him immediately.

"Tlacuache! What brings you to the depths of Mictlán, Lord of All Creatures? Did you suddenly die without my knowledge?"

"No, not at all! It's just that your last visit was several years ago. I decided to wait no longer, but to call upon you here in your own abode. I've brought you some pulque from my own royal stores. I think you'll find it quite tasty."

"Pulque? Let me try some."

And the two of them sat before the hearth and drank gourd after gourd. Soon the Xiuhtecuhtli, unaccustomed to the power of fermented aguamiel, succumbed to its effects and fell into a deep sleep, snoring contentedly.

A smile on his face, Tlacuache looked around for a bit of wood with which to carry fire back to Man. But the sun had devoured it all, so the clever opossum thought and thought until he realized what he would have to do.

Taking several more draughts of pulque to shore up his courage, he dipped his agile tail into the hearth, holding it still until the fur at its tip was blazing. Then, driven by pain and urgency, he rushed back up to the land of the living, passing the ascending sun and the spirits of warriors who guarded its rise to zenith. He reached the dwelling place of mankind and thrust his burning tail into a pile of dry wood, rekindling for his neediest subjects the flame they so desired.

Man wept for joy at the sight. He immediately set to feasting the greatness of his lord, dancing and singing hymns of praise to the magnificent, resourceful opossum.

Lord Tlacuache, nursing his now hairless tail, looked on the revelry with love and satisfaction. For now, Man was happy, and the loss of fur was a small price to pay to have brought that felicity to any creature.

The gods of the five suns soon discovered Tlacuache's theft, and in anger they rushed to the opossum's demesne, determined to end his meddlesome life.

But when they found him, he was already dead, stiff on his back, his bald tail cold as the grave.

Their anger spent, the gods muttered their mournful respects and returned to Mictlán.

And Lord Tlacuache, who had of course been playing dead the whole time, sat up and smiled at the sun.

David Bowles

FRAGMENTOS DE UNA NIÑEZ

Desde que tengo uso de razón, me he ido enterando de que soy diferente. No en la forma que siempre oímos en las películas y novelas que exponen un rebelde sin causa que busca hallarse o una pendejada por el estilo, sino que los motivos de los demás no me parecían ni lógicos ni deseables. Mi padre, un misionario y pastor evangelista, era ejemplo de lo que odiaba en los demás: seis meses del año trabajaba en los EU como mecánico, y ganaba bien. El problema era que al volver a México, él empezaba a repartir su sueldo entre sus primos, los hermanos de la iglesia y extraños, respondiendo a las quejas de mi mamá con versículos de la Biblia que exhortan bondad y abnegación. Frecuentemente invitaba a los hermanos a cenar; mi madre, mis hermanas y yo preparábamos bistec, chiles rellenos, postres, etc. Los hermanos, por supuesto, comían primero, nosotras cuando se hubieran ido, y eso de lo quedara: frijoles, arroz y tortillas.

A veces me pregunto cómo hubiera sido mi vida si mi mamá hubiera aceptado darme en adopción a aquella pareja que me vio a los dos años. Era la segunda vez que mi mamá dejaba a mi papá después de una santa golpiza (¡y eso que era cristiano!), y nos habíamos ido a vivir en un campo de tiro que le pertenecía al tío de mi mamá, quien había sido coronel en el ejército nacional y gobernador de Saltillo. Era mi costumbre construir pequeñas casas de piedra al lado de mi madre mientras que ella lavaba la ropa en tinas al aire libre. Se me caían a cada rato, y yo las volvía a construir.

Quizá esta tenacidad fue lo que le llamó la atención a la mujer que, con un arco en la mano, gritaba desesperadamente:

"Rodolfo, ¡ven! ¡Ven! ¡Mira qué bonita niña!"

Acercándose con mi mamá, le preguntó: "¿Cuántos hijos tiene?"

"Seis."

"Si me diera su hija en adopción, le daría todo, todo lo que usted no le puede dar."

"No, cómo cree."

"Le dejaríamos visitarla."

"No, es mi hija."

"La seguiría viendo. No la vamos a separar de usted."

"No, no puedo."

Mientras que la señora seguía tratando de convencer a mi mamá, su esposo en cuclillas me tocaba la cara y me sonreía.

Intentaron convencerla de que lo mejor para mí era vivir con ellos, ya que me podían dar todo lo que necesitaba para tener éxito en la vida. Le prometían que podría verme con frecuencia, que solo querían que creciera con todas las posibilidades abiertas. Bueno, claro está que mi madre se negó, aunque insistieran, y empezó a llorar. Le dijeron que estaba bien, que la dejarían en paz. Pero volvían una y otra vez para verme, con una mirada que implicaba lo mucho que me habrían dado. Cuando supe todo esto unos años después, le dije a mamá que la había regado.

"Hubiera desarrollado mis talentos al máximo, y no me hubiera olvidado de ti. Te hubiera dado todo, todo, y no estarías viviendo en la miseria como ahora."

Imagínense: mis problemas todos se hubieran atendido bien si me hubieran adoptado. La miopía, de que mis papás nunca se ocuparon, ni siquiera cuando mi maestra de segundo año se dio cuenta de que mi falta de interés se debía a que no veía el pizarrón y les mandó hablar (no asistieron a la junta); mi dislexia, que me ganó el apodo 'burra'; mi sed de saber que se iba apagando poco a poco con la mediocridad cristiana que me rodeaba. No me hubiera involucrado con el alcohol ni con el desmadre... pero en fin, así no estuvo. Por otro lado, no me arrepiento para nada de lo que he hecho, y entiendo que la mujer que soy se debe a las experiencias que tuve. Sin embargo, a veces hasta los más felices sueñan que las cosas podrían ser mejores.

Pues, mi mamá eventualmente volvió con mi papá, aunque su familia le dijo que no lo hiciera, y las cosas volvieron a ser como siempre. Vivimos un tiempo en Guadalupe, Nuevo León, allá por la colonia Tacubaya. Allí asistíamos a una iglesia Pentecostés. Después nos cambiamos a Chulavista, porque Papá vendió la tejaván donde vivíamos, y tuvimos que rentar allá.

Un día a mi hermana Verónica le tocó hacer el aseo de la iglesia; Pilar, Evangelina (una hermana de la iglesia) y yo íbamos con ella de chicle, supuestamente como ayudantes. Movimos las bancas, barrimos, trapeamos, etcétera, hasta terminar el trabajo. Cuando ya íbamos de vuelta a casa, teníamos que pasar por una calle principal. Había declives en cada costado de la carretera que bajaban hacia los terrenos que la bordeaban. Al pie de uno de estos declives íbamos caminando cuando de repente escuchamos un ruido estruendoso. Volteamos y vimos como un camión enorme se bajaba por el declive, precipitándose sobre nosotras a toda máquina. Su forma terrible estaba enmarcada por las llamaradas y oleadas de humo que se desprendían del carro con que acababa de impactarse. Corrimos como locas, cada quien por su lado. Pilar y Evangelina subieron hacia la carretera, y Verónica hacia un lado. Todas se olvidaron de mí, y yo, como tenía cuatro años y no sabía ni qué onda, me quedé con el camión balanceándose sobre mí. Y yo, corriendo a todo lo que daba, de repente, como en cada película de terror jamás vista, me caigo. Inmediatamente, algo me levanta y sigo corriendo hasta que ya no puedo más. Me paro, y en ese momento se detiene el camión.

El chofer bajó así como mareado, los ojos entreabiertos, la cabeza meneándose como si estuviera borracho, preguntando "¿estás bien?" Alguien nos dijo que los del carro habían muerto, pero después de la correteada que nos dio el camión, no quisimos ir a investigar. Regresamos a la casa, llorando todo el camino. A la noche, lo típico: dando gracias a Dios porque no nos había pasado nada, y no sé qué rollos en la iglesia, todos diciendo que fue un ángel que me salvó. Tal vez: esas cosas nunca se saben. Sólo sé que por el susto que me dio ese pinche camión, siempre me pongo nerviosa cuando algún cabrón me rebasa en la carretera.

Después de unos años, nos cambiamos al Fraccionamiento Simón Bolívar, en Monterrey. Allí pasé los anos más terribles de mi vida. Y es que mi papá había comprado un terreno al lado del de su hermano Santos, un sociópata desgraciado quien se entretenía manipulando y jodiendo a los demás.

Habíamos construido dos cuartos con techo de placa, y otro con techo de lámina. No tenían los cuartos piso, pero Papá ya había comprado el mosaico, y lo tenía afuera, junto a una ventana. Un día estaba yo jugando en el patio, construyendo una casita con los mosaicos, unos palos y pedazos de lámina, soñando, como siempre, con una casa enorme y bonita. De repente llega mi tío Santos y me ordena que me salga de ahí. Me salgo, y veo como él empieza a quebrar todos los mosaicos y a arrojarlos a su terreno para rellenarlo. Cada crujido de mosaico me era como un puñal en el corazón. Viendo las lágrimas e impotencia de mi mama, Santos dijo haciéndose el gracioso, "Al cabo, eso aquí se va a quedar. Cuando nos muramos, nada nos vamos a llevar." Pero a pesar de que nada nos íbamos a llevar, el sí rellenó su terreno con el mosaico roto de nosotros. Fue entonces cuando me empecé a dar cuenta que el sólo utilizaba la palabra de Dios para tapar su malevolencia.

Cuando llegó mi papá, mi tío, como siempre, con "la palabra de Dios" empezó a decirle que no se preocupara, que eran bienes terrenales, que al cabo él tenía un castillo en el cielo. Y yo me decía a mí misma, *está bien tener un castillo en el cielo, pero en este momento estoy en medio de la miseria, entre los cucarachos y las ratas.*

Yo ya quiero mi castillo.

Angélica Maldonado

SIRENITA, SAL DE TU OLVIDO

Me da tanta tristeza ver a la sirenita en mi lugar. Corriendo, con los ojos cerrados por las mismas malditas calles que yo sobreviví. Esa niña era tan libre, tan original, pero el monstruo le robó su identidad y la escondió entre sus ojos de ogro. Quizás por eso nunca la mira a los ojos. Para que no recuerde su viejo rostro, rostro de felicidad de química perfecta con harmonía. Como a muchas les sucede. Como a mí me sucedió.

Ahora sigo en mi lugar. En la misma jaula de oro con mi delantal, mi escoba, y el testimonio tatuado en mi espalda. Para que cuando llegue aquel día se conozca la verdad. Mi mente degenerada sale conveniente a veces. Pero nunca se me olvida por qué aguanto tanta carcajada. Y a esas copias de poco hombre les importa una chingada. ¡Qué mal pagan los hijos! Mi mente degenerada. Mi mente degenerada. Efecto de tantos años de estar encerrada.

Sirenita, mira bien en este espejo el futuro que te espera al final de este usual camino. No creas que superarte es darle tu vida a un animal a cambio de un vestido blanco, unos electrodomésticos bonitos, unos zapatos con tacón mediano, y los saludos falsos de los que te rodean. Al último ni vas a recordar quien está casada con quién, con quién engaña a quién, ni en qué trabaja el Don. Vete a realizar tus sueños. Querías ser artista, maestra, doctora o secretaria. No sé. Querías ser mujer. No galleta de jengibre que se desmorona a cada atardecer. Mereces el mundo y lo tienes a tus pies. Trágatelo. Trágate a los hombres como hongos asados con todo y salsa de empresas, academias y un poco de oficinas médicas. Esos hongos crecen en los lugares más sucios como las cantinas y bajo las piedras de infidelidad. Déjate guiar por los zumbidos de tacones altos y el choque de vidrio relleno de alcohol. O quizá están en las alturas junto a las nubes donde ellos creen estar. Lo dudo. Con extrema pasión lo dudo. Suelta ese miedo y levanta esa cabeza. Domina este mundo que desde que estabas chiquita te espera desafiar.

Yaresy Salinas

THE FOURTH QUESTION

"What does your father do?"

María froze, and her large, brown eyes stared up at her teacher. She had been placed in Ms. Dora's classroom because she could not speak English. Now, here she was, understanding English almost as well as she understood Spanish. But she wasn't prepared for this fourth question each student was being asked. She tried to concentrate, but she couldn't. María placed her bright, red crayon on her desk and placed her sweaty palms on her thin thighs. She began to nervously bite her nails as she noticed that none of the students were having any problems responding. They had answers for all four questions that the teacher was asking. What was she going to do? How could she answer the fourth question?

"Students, I would like for you to continue coloring, and answer my questions after I call your name," said Ms. Dora, who had her gray hair in a bun. María cautiously continued coloring the American flag as her teacher began to ask the questions.

"What is your mother's name?" Ms. Dora asked one of the students on her list. "Does your mother work or does she stay at home?" The student responded, and the teacher continued with the third question. "What is your father's name?"

Finally, it was María's turn to answer Ms. Dora's questions. "María, what is your mother's name?" María was able to answer that question without any problem, even though her nervousness caused her to answer in a soft, subdued voice. "Does your mother work or stay at home?" was the second question that María answered just as normally as all of her classmates. Her other was at home because they could only pick cotton during the summer and on weekends during the school year. "What is your father's name, María?"

She swallowed and answered, "Edelmiro Gonzalez." María's face turned a beet red as she tried to pronounce and spell her father's name in front of all the other students. María wished the teacher had asked the questions individually so that all the students could not hear the answers.

"What does your father do?"

"My father is not alive," María whispered.

"What did you say your father does, María?" asked the teacher.

By now, all students had stopped coloring and turned to stare at María. She could feel the tears gather in her eyes as she answered, "My father is dead."

Ms. Dora had a questioning look on her face, but she went on to the next student. María had never realized how different she would be from the other students because her father was dead.

"How was school today, María?" asked her mother that afternoon around the kitchen table as she mixed the dough for the flour tortillas.

María managed to mumble that everything was okay.

"Are you finished with your homework?" asked her mother later that evening.

When María did not respond, her mother asked, "Do you want to talk about it?" Even though María was only seven years old, her mother had always taught her to communicate to get rid of uncomfortable feelings, sadness and problems.

"Mom, Ms. Dora asked all of us some questions today. I found out that all the students in my class have a father, but I don't. I feel so embarrassed because I don't."

"María, nobody wants your father alive more than I do, but we can't change that. Why don't we practice answering the questions that your teacher asked so that you can answer without having to think about it? As you meet more students, you will learn that not all of them have fathers."

The next year, the first grade teacher had the exact same four questions as Ms. Dora did in zero grade. She asked them in the same manner and in the same order. When it was María's turn to answer the fourth question, she confidently answered, "My father is deceased."

The students wondered what the word *deceased* meant. The teacher looked at María and wondered how an eight-year-old child with limited English speaking abilities had learned to say *deceased*.

It never occurred to Ms. Dora that her questions might make a child uncomfortable.

María Ramírez

FIRST DAY

The panic began creeping into my body from the moment I pulled into the gravel parking lot at Josephina Aguilar Elementary School. Mr. Hernández, the head janitor, was out in a reflective orange vest directing the swarm of pick-ups and 70's-era gas-guzzlers, herding the students into the gym that served as a holding pen until the day officially began. The school buses pulled around back, discharging dozens more students. As I waded through the crush of students into the still-empty hallways, I felt a tension branch up through my chest cavity, into my deltoids and neck, spreading outward until it had reached my hands, which I held clenched to try and make the shaking go away.

I waited, cocooned in the safety of my classroom, for 7:45 to arrive. I set out the name tents that I'd labored to write in my best cursive; I hadn't written in cursive since junior high school, but I wanted to set a good example. When that was done, I adjusted and readjusted the desks to make sure the horseshoe was perfectly symmetrical. I was so occupied by keeping myself busy that I showed up a minute-and-a-half late to the gym. The other classes were already walking single-file down the hallway in my direction in total silence. Every student had their hands locked behind their backs like shackled inmates; later I would learn they were trained to walk that way since kindergarten to keep them from pushing and shoving in line.

When I arrived in the gym, there was only one line of students left. My class. My chest felt as though it had shrunk to half its normal size. I tried to take a deep breath and only managed a wheeze. They were just like all of the other classes, lined up perfectly, their feet on either side of a crack in the gym's blue tile. I smiled as Mr. Cantú, the coach, dismissed them to leave. They stared straight ahead. No one smiled back.

They walked to the room with military precision, just like the other classes. Not knowing whether to walk at the head or the tail of the line, I ambled along somewhere in the middle, trying to catch someone's eyes, telling myself that I wanted to reassure them. At the door's threshold, the line stopped, waiting for my permission to enter the classroom. I strode to the front, remembering that I'd planned to shake their hands on the way in.

Each student's hand felt different. Some were stiff and frigid from the air-conditioning, while others were warm and limp. I felt hands that were wet from nervousness, or dry and coarse, grimy-feeling. When everyone had found their name tent and settled into their assigned desk, I looked out and all I saw was a faceless sea of children. I rubbed my eyes, as if the problem were me not seeing straight. The sweat from my hands stung. It seemed odd that I could so clearly differentiate their hands, but that their faces all swam together. So many eyes.

I held up a piece of chalk, hoping they wouldn't see my hand shaking. I wrote my name on the blackboard, slowly and deliberately, trying not to let the lines tremble. Mr. Walsh. It looked foreign written there, like a character from a nineteenth century novel.

I looked back up at the eyes. Every student sat with their back straight, their hands set in front of them on their desks. I cleared my throat. My mouth felt dry, insufficiently lubricated for words to squeeze out. I tapped my name on the board insistently with the chalk, as if trying to prove to myself that it were indeed my name. "Good morning, boys and girls," I managed, finally, just as I'd practiced. "My name is Mr. Walsh."

I was twenty-two years old, just out of college. Only a week earlier, I'd made the twenty-eight hour drive from Minnesota to Edinburg, Texas. I'd gone from living with my parents, passing myself off as an unemployed writer for a summer, to living in my grandfather's vacant Winnebago trailer at the Cactus Gardens RV Park. It was his idea that I come here; he'd been arguing all along that I needed to get a real job. "All you need is a pulse," he told me, when I protested that I was in way, shape or form qualified to teach elementary students. "The schools down there are growing faster than corn in July." A month later, I found myself in deep South Texas, teaching at a country school surrounded by acre after acre of nothing but scrub brush.

The first activity I'd planned was coming up with the classroom rules. I decided not to post the rules in advance, but rather to solicit the student's input and build the rules by classroom consensus. I'd seen a video on-line of a teacher doing this. She called on students one at a time from the multitude of raised hands, and they offered suggestions such as "no pinching" and "no tattletaling" which she expertly rephrased into positive-sounding "classroom expectations."

"We're going to start with a rule-building exercise," I said. "Who would like to volunteer a classroom rule for us?" One hand went up.

"Yes?" I said. I looked at the name tent on the student's desk. Ramón Garza. "What rule would you like to contribute?"

"Be respectful toward one another," he said. I wrote it up on the blackboard, unsure how to proceed, since it had already been stated as a positive expectation. "Good," I said. "What else?" I looked out at the rest of the eyes and waited for the hands to start shooting up. The students remained seated, looking as expressionless and about as animated as Lego people.

Only one hand was raised. It was still Ramón Garza. I noticed that he wasn't sitting like the rest of the students.

His legs were crossed underneath his desk, his feet not flat on the floor like the rest. As I surveyed the rest of the room, his hand began surging higher in the air, then oscillating back and forth wildly. "Sir, ooh, ooh me, sir," he said. "Call on me." I waited for the rest of the students to follow his lead, but they ignored him completely. It didn't occur to me yet that his eagerness to answer didn't just express his zeal for learning, but also social awkwardness, a kind of ignorance—either naïve or intentional—of the unwritten codes that governed the lives of the students of Josefina Aguilar. One of those rules was *don't talk in class on the first day.*

I didn't want to call on any of the other students, for fear of making them feel uncomfortable. I called on Ramón again. "Be courteous at all time to teachers and staff," he said. I wrote down the second suggestion on the board as well. This wasn't working as it had in the video. If no one else was going to talk, couldn't Ramón at least form his rules in the negative, so I could have something to rephrase?

Ramón's hand continued to be raised, but I pretended not to see it. I wanted to be sure not to let any one student dominate the classroom conversation.

"Thank you so much for your thoughts," I said to Ramón, finally. "Can we hear from someone else now?"

Ramón let his hand drop down to his desk grudgingly. I tapped the chalk against the blackboard. When I couldn't take the silence anymore, I blurted out, "What about *no fighting?*" Ramón nodded approvingly, but the rest of the class remained stoic. "Or better yet, what if I put *respect each other's actions?* How does that sound?"

No one objected, or agreed, either. "Does that make you think of anything else?" I asked. I wiped sweat from my forehead with the sleeve of my hunter-green dress shirt, recently purchased at the Pharr Goodwill. "Nothing? How about, 'no name-calling?'" My eyes met Ramón's, who was shaking his head vigorously. I tried to resist the temptation to just look at him, since he was the only one whose gaze didn't seem to go straight through me into the wall. "Can I put 'respect other's words?' That way it won't seem like these are things we're not supposed to do. Instead, we can think about them as helpful reminders."

I looked up at the clock. It was only 8:35. There were still six hours to fill before the end of the day.

I was an English major in college, and I dreamed of being a writer, even if all I'd eked out in a summer spent in my parents' basement were a few convoluted paragraphs saturated in existential angst. Still, writing was the subject I was most excited about teaching. During my phone interview for the position, Mr. Villarreal had been excited as well, because at the end of the year the students were tested by the state on their ability to write a personal narrative. At the Wal-Mart in Edinburg, I'd bought black and white Mead composition notebooks for each student. After my failed attempt at rule-building, I walked around the horseshoe handing them out, trying not to show my worry that they wouldn't like them. There had been so many notebooks to choose from, ones with neon colors and Dragonball-Z and My Little Pony. I'd picked the simplest ones because I wanted the students to be able to decorate them in a way that said something about who they were. But what if they thought I wasn't excited to teach them, seeing Puritanical black-and-white gifts? At first, my fears seemed to be confirmed. They set the notebooks down on their desks and didn't open them as I finished making my way around the room.

Finally, a student raised his hand. It was Ramón Garza, of course.

"Can we keep them?" he asked breathlessly. I nodded. "They're free, sir? Really?"

His hands passed lightly over the cover. I studied the rest of the room. Several students waited with pencils poised over the blank space underneath the word *name*, waiting for my instructions.

"I'm giving them to you on one condition," I said to Ramón. He let his hand drop off the notebook onto his lap. "Don't you want to know what that condition is?' I asked. He nodded skeptically. "The condition is that you write in them every morning. Do you think you can do that?"

"Yes, sir," he said, recovering his previous enthusiasm.

"Later on, we'll have time to decorate them however you like," I said, looking out at the entire class. "But for now I want to get started writing. How many people have written a letter before?" No one looked at me. "How many people have gotten a letter before, in the mail?" Blank stares. Only later would I realize that some of the students' parents couldn't read or write; others lived in *colonias* with no sewage or running water, let alone regular mail service.

"That's okay," I said, walking to the board. I wrote the day's date at the top in cursive: *August 15, 2003*. Then, underneath, *Dear Mr. Walsh*.

"Can you copy this down on the first page of your notebook?" The students dug into their backpacks for pencils and pens. "Now, I want you to write to me and introduce yourself. I'll give you twenty minutes. All right?"

No one wrote, except Ramón Garza, who grinned at me as I walked past his desk and saw that he was already on page two. The rest of the students stared at their blank pages, shifting nervously in their seats. A general feeling of confusion filled the air.

Okay, I pep-talked myself, you can do this. I navigated from desk to desk, asking questions in a voice loud enough so that other students could overhear. *What do you like to do? How many people are in your family? Tell me about them. Tell me as much as you can.*

Two or three pencils started moving, trying out a few preliminary words. Then a few more followed suit. Once they broke through that initial barrier, I saw that several students filled up pages as effortlessly as breathing. But most of them toiled over every letter, gripping their pencils ferociously, squeezing the words out of them like the final dollop of toothpaste from the tube.

I circulated around the inside of the horseshoe, offering encouragement and seeing what they'd done so far. Everyone, I noticed, wrote in print. More than a few students composed in all capital letters, spacing three or four words out over the course of a line, or writing in towering script that filled up four lines per letter. Students spelled words phonetically, replacing "I" with "Ay," or, more perplexingly, "Eye." There were two or three students whose writing I was unable to decipher at all, seemingly just a series of unconnected letters, not separated by any spaces. As I circulated around the classroom, I smiled enthusiastically to conceal my shock. I was asking them to introduce themselves, and half of them could barely write a complete sentence.

I might have realized at that moment, on the very first day, that I was in way over my head at Josefina Aguilar. I was a first-year teacher. I spoke only limited Spanish. I didn't have the slightest idea where to begin to help them. But I was either too brave or too ignorant to see that. Instead, I found the anxiety that had gripped my shoulders and my lungs all morning slowly begin to subside, replaced by a newfound sense of purpose. Writing was something that was important, and it was something I knew about. Who better than me to introduce them to its emancipative power?

In spite of the students' difficulties, there was something peaceful about the sound of graphite working across mashed-up tree pulp. The concentration of each student pooled and cohered until we were surrounded by a small lake of it, each pencil a current in a fluid choreography of thought.

The aura of calm was interrupted by a knock on the door. It was repeated three times, a little louder than really seemed necessary. "Keep working," I said, as I went to the door. His face was pressed against the window, his nose and cheeks flattened against the glass.

"Good morning," I said. "Can I help you?"

He was a tall boy, bigger by a head than any of the other boys in the classroom. His face seemed older too, his features sharper and more defined. "Are you the sir?" he asked. His dark eyes met mine and did not let go, an invitation to a staring contest.

"Your name must be Eduardo Santos," I said, since his was the only desk currently unoccupied.

"No it's not, *sir*," he said. The way he said it, the *sir* sounded like an insult to knighthood.

"Are you looking for Mr. Walsh's class?"

"My name is *Eddie*."

I met his glare with what I hoped was an inviting smile. "Perfect. Welcome to class, Eddie. I'm glad you made it. We're just getting started. We're writing letters to introduce ourselves."

"I already did. I'm Eddie."

The rest of the class had turned their eyes toward us. I noticed that the two girls on either side of Eddie's empty desk, Gladys Gómez and Yesenia Solís, shifted their chairs slightly to give him more space. The students, who had hunched their backs over their notebooks, straightened back up.

"Oh, I'm sure there's a lot more to know," I said. I walked him to his desk. I picked up the name tent and folded it the other way, pulling out the Sharpie that had been tumbling around in my breast pocket. *Eddie*, I wrote. "There, now that's your seat."

"Does it belong to me, sir?" It took me a second to grasp what he was getting at.

"I guess it belongs to the school. Consider it on loan for a while."

"Okay, *sir*."

I handed Eddie his journal. "Just tell me everything about yourself you want me to know."

"What if there are things you don't want to know?"

I liked Eddie Santos from the start. I knew from that moment on that he would be a handful. But I liked that about him, even as I felt a vague sense of fear at the same time. Unlike his classmates, I thought, he had a healthy distrust of authority. He didn't care what anybody else thought, or at least that's what he wanted us to believe.

I left fifteen minutes at the end of the day to pass out the spelling books. Initially, I hadn't been crazy about the idea of teaching spelling, my own least favorite subject in school. In the era of dictionary.com and spell-check, it seemed like an anachronism. But seeing the kinds of problems the students were having with their writing, I had to concede that the requirement probably made sense.

The students were completing a math pre-test, working silently at their desks. I walked over to the cabinet at the back of the room and opened the door, not really paying attention to what I was doing. Ever since the writing exercise, I felt emboldened. I knew I could do this. More than that, I knew I wanted to do this. I had to keep myself from daydreaming too much about what the coming weeks would bring, social studies projects and poetry and journals that had to be replaced because they contained too few pages.

I found the bright yellow spelling books on the top shelf. I reached my hand up to see if there was any way I could get them to slide down, but they were too high up. I looked around for something to stand on. All the desks were occupied, except mine, which was too big to drag over to the cabinet. Checking to make sure I wasn't distracting the students, I rolled the swivel chair from behind my desk next to the cabinet. I stepped up on the seat and felt the wheels turn to adjust to my weight. Pulling down a stack of five spelling books, I got down from the chair. I walked to the open end of the horseshoe, quietly laying the books on the corners of students' desks.

I repeated this process until there were only five more books left to distribute. Back up on the chair, I heard a *click-click-click* sound that seemed to originate from the back of the cabinet. Instinctively I turned and looked at Eddie, but he was sitting with his forehead on the desk. Ignoring the sound, I pulled the remaining books from the cabinet. I saw the rattlesnake coiled behind the last stack of books. At first I couldn't believe what I was seeing. When I closed my eyes and re-opened them, it was still there.

I felt the books dropping from my hands, landing with a dull thud and scattering across the floor. Losing my balance, I jumped to the floor as the chair rolled across the back of the classroom. In response to the noise, the snake tumbled out of the cabinet, landing on the linoleum and squirting to the center of the classroom. Gladys Gómez was the first one to see it. She let out a shriek, which quickly echoed across the room. Students scooted away, desks, chairs and all. The metal tips of the desk legs screeched across the newly-waxed tile.

Everyone moved except the student nearest the snake. She sat at her desk, like a small island, in the center of the classroom. In the confusion, her name tent had fallen on the floor. The snake had left me separated from my seating chart. She remained silent as the snake flicked its tongue in and out at her, staring back at the snake. Later I would find out that her name was Letty Arévalo. She'd been diagnosed with autism by the school psychologist the previous year. She read at a first grade level and almost never spoke.

"Don't move," I said. Wasn't it true that snakes didn't strike if you remained perfectly motionless? "Everyone stay as still as you can."

The *click-click-click* of its tail reverberated through the room. I felt extremely light-headed. I thought I might throw up. A snake in the classroom was not something I'd thought to prepare for, even in the worst case scenarios I was prone to imagining at night.

My first instinct was to look around for something to kill it with. I briefly entertained the thought of the heavy metal Swinger stapler on my desk, only a few yards away.

But what if I missed? What if the force of the blow wasn't enough to kill it and the snake decided to retaliate? I could scream for help. I could grab Letty and move her out of harm's way. I could maneuver to the front of the room and press the red emergency button that would connect me to the office. This last option surely would have been the calm, rational, responsible thing to do, but some impulse seized me up. Instead of asking for help from the outside world, I headed toward Letty's desk, putting myself halfway in between the snake and her frozen body.

It might have been a heroic move, even, had I not frozen up immediately also. Somewhere I'd heard that snakes only struck when coiled. Until that moment, the snake had remained more or less elongated across the white tile, as though sunning itself beneath the fluorescent lights. It chose the instant that I approached to slither into its deadly halo. I felt its beady eyes fixed on me. My knees began to buckle.

"Don't move, don't move, don't move," I repeated over and over like a mantra, more for my benefit than that of the students. Not that I needed to say it. My legs were putty. My heart beat through my shirt. I was hostage in the center of my own classroom, on the very first day of school.

That was the way they found us when Mr. Hernández walked into the room a few seconds later carrying a sharp-tipped shovel. A boy from the neighboring class had looked inside our room on his way to the bathroom, then run back to his teacher, who *had* buzzed the office.

The janitor strode deliberately to Letty's desk, his movement almost supernaturally fast against the backdrop of our paralyzed suspension. He lifted the shovel high above his head. When it dropped, it made a clean break, rust brown blood oozing across the stainless tile. Without saying a word, Mr. Hernández set down the shovel and leaned over and picked up the two pieces, head and tail. The head was still writhing slightly in his hand. Later, I heard in the teacher's lounge that he'd taken the snake in his pick-up and thrown the pieces out the window in a vacant lot a few miles from the school. The other teachers said it was to guard against the old adage that one snake attracts another.

After Mr. Hernández left, silence filled the room. I was afraid to speak, knowing how my voice would tremble like a radio station that refused to come in all the way.

"Is everyone okay, Mr. Walsh?" The voice belonged to the principal, Mr. Villarreal, who was stepping in from the doorway. His nasal voice bounced against the walls, decaying into a faint echo. He stopped next to Letty's desk.

I surveyed the wreckage, the crush of chairs and desks tilted every which way, where only moments before perfect order and symmetry had reigned. "I think so," I said.

He paused for a moment, then apparently was satisfied. "Is everything all right, *mija*?" he asked Letty. He stood stiffly beside her, unaccustomed to providing comfort. She nodded meekly, although her face had not begun to regain its color.

"Some excitement on the first day, boys and girls," he said. I smiled, hoping that was the reaction he wished to illicit. "Everyone help Mr. Walsh get things back in order, okay? We've all seen snakes before. Let's get back to work. *¿Está bien?*"

Letty Arévalo waited until he'd left the classroom to burst into tears. She buried her face in the front of her white blouse.

"All right," I said, letting out a deep breath. I realized that I wasn't going to do much better at offering comfort. I put a hand tentatively on her shoulder. "No one's hurt. Everything's going to be okay."

The students, more composed than I was, began to drag the desks back into the horseshoe I'd so carefully constructed. Ramón Garza volunteered to help pass out the textbooks that were all over the floor. I assigned a student to escort Letty, who looked on the verge of passing out, to the nurse's office. I gave another student the bathroom pass to get paper towels. When she returned, I got down on my hands and knees and cleaned up the snake blood on the tile myself.

At last we were ready to begin again, the desks reset, the textbooks distributed, the students' names inscribed in blue or black ink in the front inside covers, the condition marked as *excellent*. I looked up at the clock at the front of the room. There was barely a minute left to go in the day.

I looked out at the class. There was a hand raised in the back of the classroom. I swallowed.

"Yes, Eddie," I said.

"That was cool, sir," he responded, a smirk spreading across his face. "Is everyday going to be like this?"

Daniel Tyx

CODE BLACK

Teacher's lives have many twists and turns. Those who seem to be the sheep of the fold take the place of the shepherd from time to time, as if to give us a life lesson and remind us that we teachers are only human beings and—most importantly—instruments of God. One unexpected experience made me change forever the false image I had of what a teacher should be.

"Attention teachers, students, and everybody in the building: this is a code black. I repeat, this is a code black," the principal announced on the intercom, her voice as clear and calmed as a lake.

Oh, my God, I thought, my mind going blank, my body paralyzed. *What are we supposed to do?*

It was my first year as a teacher, and only one month had gone by. I had been assigned to a 2nd grade class, and I was learning little by little. Not everything comes with a manual, so you pick up some things in training and some others with experience, but the truth is, there will always be something else to learn. At this time I was unfamiliar with the code black process since I had just arrived from another country where this is not the practice. Nobody had really taken the time to explain to me what it was or what to do if a threatening situation arose.

Despite my shock, I suddenly remembered a co-teacher telling me over lunch time a few days before, "If you hear a code black warning, lock your classroom door and tell the kids to hide."

So I did. "Kids, don't panic!" I yelled in the midst of all their commotion and alarmed voices, trying in vain to hide the terror that was so obviously revealed in my voice. "Please hide under the desk tables while I lock the door."

As all this was happening in a flash, a million images and memories were rolling in slow motion in my mind, just like in a film. I started to remember how, when I decided to become a teacher, I had felt I possessed all the qualities a person needed to be an excellent educator. I thought I was knowledgeable enough to enlighten children's lives. I thought I was sufficiently generous to share everything I was with them. Oh, God... how mistaken I was! In that very moment I felt I was anything but qualified, knowledgeable or generous enough to stand for these children.

After locking the door, I turned back. Though I could have sworn the classroom had been deserted, then their frightened whispers and sobbing cut through the silence. I hid myself below a table with some of the children. My heart was beating terribly fast; my hands were sweaty and shaky. I tried to calm them down with no luck; of course, they could sense my fear.

Suddenly I heard someone calling in a whisper from across the classroom, "Pssst, Miss: you forgot to turn off the lights!" I instantly jumped from under the table and ran towards the switch to turn it off. I felt like one of those soldiers in combat movies, in the midst of war, running unprotected across a battlefield.

I returned victorious to my hideout and tried to comfort my students by saying with an optimistic tone, "Okay, everything is all right now; nobody will see us."

But then I heard two other voices coming from beneath the tables by the windows. "Miss Hernandez, the curtains, we need to pull them down," said one voice. Then the other asked "Can I close them?"

That was not good! What other risks was I overlooking? I couldn't believe how much my ignorance about the procedure was exposing my students! I wasn't sure what to respond to their questions; I was analyzing the situation when all of a sudden I saw them climbing over the tables to reach the string of the curtains to roll them down. Maybe my bewildered expression gave them the courage to be the heroes, risking themselves to protect their classmates and their astonished teacher.

Well, after all the stress, at least we all felt safer now that we were not visible to potential threats. But this feeling didn't last long; someone twisted the knob and slightly opened the door... I hadn't locked it after all! Words cannot describe what I felt in that moment; only those who have experienced this level of menace—not for oneself, but for the little ones whose safety God has conferred to you—can understand. The students felt the same terror. We all turned to look at each other, and we held hands even tighter. Some of them cried out for their mothers, some others shed tears, and definitely all of us were shaking in mortal fear. Nothing entered the room, not even a hand, a face, a weapon... nothing. The suspense was killing us!

At that moment, via the intercom, a voice that sounded to me like the chant of an angel (given the situation) announced, "Code green, code green. Teachers and students, you can now resume your activities."

I was so relieved that everything had gone back to normal! Of course I wanted to find out what had happened and make sure there was no more menace for the students, but for now I was thankful and pleased. Then the same voice—not sounding at all like an angel this time—added, "This was just a trial. Thanks for your cooperation."

Mónica G. Hernández

UNEXPLAINABLE PHENOMENON

Most folks, if given the chance, will spend their summer completing projects, reading books, having family time, or traveling. Like most people in education, I did all of that my first summer off. I had many tough jobs before working for a school. This was the first job where eight weeks were given just like that. The first few weeks I spent reading various books I had purchased that year. But soon, to put it mildly, I really ran out of things to do.

I guess I was not used to the free time. My prior work experience came with a sort of hustle and bustle. Like the proverb *busy hands are not idle hands,* my workload helped each day grow short. But now my freedom altered that habit. As it was summer, my days grew long *literally.* By the middle of my holiday experience, my routine changed. I had become a nocturnal being. I spent many late night hours enjoying various readings and classic cinema. Should I choose Betty Davis or Joan Crawford? Will I do poetry or short stories?

One of those late nights I decided to take in the breeze. It must have been about three in the morning. I was admiring the starlit sky, basking in the moonbeams that drew the essence of the night to my porch. How peaceful summer nights tend to be.

From a distance I heard the *clop-clop* of a horse trotting toward our home. The sound kept getting louder and louder. Whatever was approaching came closer and closer. It was not uncommon where I live to see skillful horse riders pass their merry way. I myself enjoy riding on occasion. Nonetheless, I did think that the timing was a little odd. What person rides at three in the morning? People up at this time are possibly throwing newspapers or making donuts. Maybe this individual had an appointment. Perhaps he or she was riding to work early on the horse. I knew that my dog Skippy would bark away, so naturally I waited for her performance as watchdog to begin. Right on the money she began to sound her canine warning. The trotting got louder and closer.

At last the sound met the illumination of our security light. To my surprise nothing appeared. I could hear the clatter of hooves trotting along. But nothing was there. For a moment I questioned my senses. Were my eyes and ears deceiving me? Skipper my dog was barking away at the sound as well. Was I crazy? I got up from my rocking chair to approach the desolate road.

Without hesitation I advanced toward the anomaly. The sound of the horse trotting stopped dead at our gate. Skipper was on duty with me. There we were, both of us looking at nothing. I could hear a horse moving, breathing. From time to time I could sense the horse picking up a front leg and dropping it on the vacant dirt road. There was an unsettling sound of clip-clops, as if hooves struck rocks, but nothing was there. To my further surprise it sounded like the horse was throwing its head up as if to get its mane or flies out of its eyes.

I once again peered into sheer darkness. I felt certain that some entity was luring me with fascination, taunting my sight.

My thoughts were in chaos. In Spanish I called out, "Éste no es un lugar de descanso. Usted necesita encontrar el lugar para descansar. Esta casa es del señor Jesús Cristo. Usted necesita estar en paz, así que por favor vaya a descansar."

I then repeated my message in English: "This is not a resting place. You need to find the right place to rest. This is a house of our lord Jesus Christ. You need to be at peace, so please find it so you may rest."

With whose words the entity appeared to plunge back into the abyss of darkness from which it came. Mind you there was nothing, absolutely nothing. I saw with my ears and not my eyes. My dog and I stared at the barren road. With relief we could hear the trotting of the nothingness grow further and further away. Just as the light that first hits at dawn to create the horizon, the sound was finally gone. In essence the darkness was at last dispersed.

I slowly turned and headed back to that protected haven, our porch. As I walked, I came to the conclusion that our porch was not the safe sanctuary: my *faith* kept me protected. The idea that I needed protection was preposterous. I was raised to fear God and nothing else. As with a child, when darkness came, fear took over. Fear losses its potency with time and age. My faith in God, I realized, had grown stronger than any light, ghost chasers, or sprit mediums available. I had no need for such things. I had my faith.

At day break I retold my encounter to my family. They believed me, which was no surprise since things sometimes do go bump in the night.

Many summers have since passed. I still keep my routine of books, cinema and dark early mornings of chilled air. Of course, you can always buy good books or see good movies. But you can never get that early morning air bottled in any air freshener.

My faith still grows strong. Prayer is good for the soul.

I recount this event to anyone who cares to listen as a form of storytelling. Many believe me; others do not. The paranormal treads a thin line between fantasy and reality, maybe only a hop, skip, and a jump away. I'm sure we have all had some kind of unexplainable phenomenon happen to us. If it has not come to pass for you, hang around my place. Eerie sounds of trotting can occasionally lead to roads of pure faith.

Félix Omar Vela

THE PULGA

Yawning, I fought the urge to drop my head the entire drive. The only thing keeping me awake was the thrill of a new experience. Glancing at my mother's face in the rear view mirror, I knew she didn't share my excitement. Her face was hard, and those black eyes stayed stony the entire drive, except for those rare occasions when the stones melted into glistening pools of water that ran down her face then disappeared forever. The sun had not yet risen, yet my stomach was wide awake and burning with hunger. But I would've starved before complaining to that face in the rear view mirror.

Finally the car came to a stop with dust whirling all around it from the loose gravel and dirt that covered the entire lot. We were early enough to get a good spot, so we chose a corner booth near the entrance next to the fruit vendor. Then in silence we began to unload the trunk. I found a box small enough to wrap my arms around and made my way back to the booth. Setting the box down on our table, I pushed back the flaps. My breath caught in my lungs as I peered into the box and saw Baby Horse inside. I don't know how long I've had Baby Horse, but there are pictures of him in my crib. I picked him up and was headed back to the car, hoping to sneak him onto the backseat where he'd be safe from capitalism, but instead turned around just in time to watch my mother speed off towards the main road. "Stop messing with those toys and finish unpacking! Customers will be here soon!" my sister shouted at me.

When I finished pulling the last of the heavy boxes to our booth, since my pregnant sister Alicia insisted it was "bad for the baby," (her new favorite phrase, which meant she didn't ever have to do anything), I began arranging them on the table.

"Just make a big heap; people can dig around if they really want something," she complained from the lawn chair where she had sprawled out to rest. I ignored her and continued with my work, putting the largest *peluches* in the back row, the smallest ones up front, primping the doll's hair, and straightening my bunny's ears. When I was done, it looked like a class picture. I felt proud: after all, heaps were for garbage.

As the sun rose so did the heat.

"Here's some money; grab a few cokes. And don't be shy: ask for the change, okay?" My sister shoved a five-dollar bill in my pocket. I ignored her remark, grateful just to get away for a few minutes. Making my way towards the *lonchería,* I felt someone staring at me. A blonde girl sitting in a pickup truck filled with bubblegum waved, and I walked towards the truck.

"Hi, I'm Cassie. What's your name?" she asked me.

"Eva." I looked past her at the mountain of gum.

"What are you doing here?" she probed.

"Came to sell my toys," I answered, feeling my chin raise slightly as said it.

"That's crazy. Why would anyone do that?" As if selling gumballs out of a pickup truck wasn't weird at all.

"'Cause my sister's gonna have a baby, and diapers are expensive," I realized with chagrin how much I sounded like my mother. "How much for a gum?" I suddenly didn't want to be there anymore.

"A quarter."

I dug into my pocket for some change, took the gum, and hurried off to find the lonchería.

"What took you so long?" Alicia demanded as I handed her a coke.

"I stopped to buy some gum: look..." I opened my mouth wide to show off my dark purple tongue.

"Disgusting," she muttered and went back to her magazine.

"*PELUCHES UN DÓLAR!*" I yelled every time someone with a kid walked by. The baby dolls sold quickly, but I kept a nervous eye on Baby Horse. A small boy about four years old approached the table. It looked like he maybe had a cold because his face was sticky with snot all over; I wrinkled my own nose in disgust. He picked up a few *peluches* then tossed them carelessly back on the table before walking away. I jumped off the chair and immediately began to rearrange them, watching my sister, who was beginning to doze off in a shady corner. I looked back at Baby Horse sitting in the back row: he was frightened. I looked back at my sister: the Tweetie Bird on her shirt was stretched and deformed over her growing belly.

"I hate you," I whispered to Tweetie. I grabbed a *peluche* and shoved it under my t-shirt to see what I would look like and then quickly put it back as a large group of customers were heading towards us.

Among the crowd was a young girl about fifteen with a perfectly rounded belly just like my sister's. My heart froze as she looked at the toys, hand over belly. I knew what she would pick for her baby. I couldn't let this happen!

"Slut!" I blurted out. The look of pain on her face matched her reaction as she dropped Baby Horse like a fireball. She ran off with her hands still wrapped around her, tears streaming. My eyes followed her as she exited the pulga where my mother's car was making its way back in.

"Time to go," I said, shaking Alicia till she opened her eyes.

"Did we have a good day?" she asked looking over at the nearly empty table.

"We had a great day."

Evangelina Ayon

EDUCATION IN TRYING TIMES

I was born in 1921 in Morgan City, Mississippi. I started school at a very early age, attending class at a one-room log cabin school on the outskirts of town. Now, this wasn't precisely the norm back then, but my aunt was the school teacher, and she knew Mama needed time away from me. I was the youngest of a large family, lots of mouths to feed and bodies to clothe, so the truth was that Mama didn't just want a break: she also needed to go to work.

She worked a spell in a small grocery store, but my father was a jealous husband, and he couldn't handle the thought of so many men having the chance to interact with his wife day in and day out. But even though Mama only had a second-grade education, she was a brilliant, self-taught woman, and she quickly found work as an English tutor for Chinese immigrants in town. My father didn't fuss too much about this new job—he reckoned she'd not get fresh with Chinamen.

Though I loved school, learning to read quickly and helping my aunt with the younger pupils, by the spring of 1927 the log-cabin school was no more. I lived in the rich land of the delta, in Mississippi, and we were surrounded by rivers and lakes: the Mississippi, Yazoo, Big Black. Well, the rain started to fall that spring, and it didn't stop. Finally, the levees broke in the night. My father woke with water in his bed. We got up just as we were and managed to get onto the roof of our house. The house was just sitting on blocks, so we began floating. We were crying, cold, hungry, and as dawn was just breaking I saw two chickens on the roof with us. We all got a big laugh. I know we were a strange sight to the soldiers coming to our rescue. The house was almost under water, and the soldiers got us into the boats in the nick of time. Almost everyone living in that area lost all they had. The Army set up tents and provided for us about three months, until we could relocate. Worse thing of all was that we were saved just in time to go through the Great Depression!

As my family got through the natural disasters and into the darkness of the early 1930s, government programs made themselves felt in the lives of students. There was a government program to give material to make clothing for the needy. About every three months we all were given whatever material there was a surplus of. This one time there was only one color: pink with flowers. No other choice. The following few days we all began to show up at school, girls with pink dresses, and boys with pink shirts. No one poked fun at anyone else, as we all were in the same boat.

I doubt if you've ever worn 'flour-sack' underwear. Our flour came in sturdy cloth bags, so they were ripped apart and washed. Our mothers would make undies out of them. Most of the sacks had 'XXX' on them and my mother usually put that part in the back. Salt and sugar also came in cloth bags. We made some beautiful handkerchiefs out of them. A little lace and embroidering made them treasures.

I was eleven years old before I tasted an orange or grapefruit. The U.S. Government sent a trailer-truckload to our school. We got two or three of each. I say on the bench, staring at the strange fruit. I didn't know how to eat them. After a spell, I just punched a hole in the orange and sucked the juice. The grapefruit I was scared to eat. The home-room teacher told us to peel them and eat the sections: I didn't like mine and threw it away.

I can't talk to you about education back then without telling you about Miss Martin! She was our principal in grammar school. That school was new to me, and everyone told me bad things about Miss Martin. She was our home-room teacher also. One day, while supposedly studying, I was drawing Miss Martin's picture. I really had her looking ugly: buck teeth, long nose, messy hair, the works. I didn't know, but she was standing quietly behind me, watching my masterpiece. I also included a poem about her that did nothing for her image.

When I finished she quietly tapped me and whispered, "Stay after school. We need to talk." No one else heard her. She didn't make any scene. I could just see her expelling me or worse. But no. She was so tender and sweet to me... I just cried. She saved my life that year. I was just about dead with malnutrition, was fainting at my desk. She had the county health nurse look me over. Miss Martin put me in the cafeteria chopping onions, tomatoes, lettuce and pick-ing up trays, with orders to the other workers to give me all I could eat and let me take food home. This wonderful teach-er became the best friend I've ever had.

Soon we had soup kitchens and bread lines to stand in to get food. All around, people were fainting because they were hungry. I know God had His hand on us. Young peo-ple today, I tell them to take advantage of the chance they've got to have a good education. I'm sure very few if any of them go to school sick from hunger. There are so many wonderful opportunities around them... and in the world of today, an education is a must. I always said this little rhyme to my children:

> Rise up, study hard
> Do not ever shirk your work
> For well I know
> And so do you
> That anyone can be a jerk.

There's something about hard times that makes you appreciate the value of a free, public education. Too many people are losing sight of that today.

Lois Marie Garza

ESCAPING THE ICE

Oasis swam away from the educational building quickly, hoping not to be confronted by the other students again. She couldn't bear to be humiliated once more. The cold Europan water rushed through her gills as she took shallow, shaky breaths. Oasis saw her surroundings begin to blur as she sped up. She hit her top speed and felt relief wash over her. There was no way the bullies could catch her now, because she was the fastest swimmer in the whole city.

After she was only a few miles from home, Oasis slowed and stopped by the small forest made of aquatic plants native to Europa to rest. After deciding to perch in the branches of an odd, tree-like plant, she began to rummage in her pack of school supplies and took out a notebook made of electrostatic plastic sheets. Using her stylus, Oasis started working on a new design of her spaceship since her teacher had confiscated her previous blueprint. This version was more streamlined and seemed able to escape Jupiter's gravitational pull, unlike her first few attempts. Oasis looked over it again and seemed pleased. Perhaps her "silly fantasies" about leaving this little moon and exploring different worlds would finally come true.

She closed her notebook and put it away. It was probably best if she went home now, so her father wouldn't begin worrying about her.

Oasis opened the front door of her house and peered in. Her father (whose Europan name can be roughly translated "Turbo") was pacing—or actually swimming—up and down the room, until he saw her. Then he seemed to relax a little, but his face was stern.

"Where were you, Oasis? I was worried!" he said as he pulled Oasis into the house.

"Well, I was working on a little spaceship design again, and I kind of lost track of time... sorry Dad," Oasis mumbled as she took out her notebook and showed her father the blueprint.

He examined it for a moment, then said, awestruck, "I see why you lost track of time. This one's beautiful... You must have put an enormous amount of effort into it."

Oasis flushed at the unexpected compliment and changed the subject abruptly. "Er... what's for dinner?"

"Just the usual... Only slightly burnt," Her father said before he strode into the kitchen, remembering to take the food out of the sealed oven that cooked using metallic sodium. He came back with a covered magnetic dish of burnt fish and some other alien plant that's the equivalent of broccoli on Earth. Oasis sat down at one of the chairs as her father put down the plate of food in the center of the small table, where it clung with a hollow click. She pulled a few burnt fish from under the covered plate and began eating, not bothered by the charred meat.

"Come on, eat your veggies!" her father insisted, forking a clump of the green plant into Oasis's clamp-like eating utensil. She sighed and nibbled a bit of the vegetable and quickly returned to gnawing at the tough, burnt meat of the fish.

"So, how's your project to find life on other planets going, Dad?" Oasis said after she finished eating, hoping he had found even the smallest bit of evidence.

"I still haven't found anything," he sighed, a wrinkle forming in between the area his eyebrows would have been if he had them.

"I want to help you look for some evidence then." Oasis decided. Turbo agreed, as long as Oasis helped him clean up the mess they had left on the table.

After they finished cleansing the table, they swam to the lab, which was full of complicated equipment and machines. They waited impatiently at the device that picked up many different types and frequencies of signals to check if anything came up.

"I think we might need some *golub*," Oasis's dad said after about an hour of waiting, referring to a coffee-like goop that helped Europans keep alert. "You stay here and call me if a signal reaches us, okay?"

"All right," Oasis replied. She idled about near the contraption and traced random patterns onto her tail fin for a while, when suddenly bizarre noises burst out of the speaker for radio signals. Oasis was frozen with shock. The sounds were very different compared to anything from her moon. The Europans had a language that resembled water, while the melody coming from the machine was exciting and upbeat. Then Oasis remembered she was supposed to call her father when she received a transmission, so she let out a little yelp in the general direction of the kitchen.

WHAM! Oasis's father burst in, tumbling through the doorway somewhat like the ninjas on Earth, managing not to spill even the smallest drop of *golub*, and halted when he was next to Oasis.

"We've got a signal?" he asked enthusiastically, while handing a warm cup of the goopy substance to Oasis. She nodded slowly, still stupefied by the signal and her father's odd performance. His fingers flew across the keyboard installed into the front of the machine, in order to trace the transmission. An image of a blue and green planet appeared on the screen, and data on a corner of the screen showed that there were also other kinds of signals coming from satellites around the planet. Oasis's father switched to the digital signal and got into the huge data stream humans called "the Internet". Oasis and her dad spent the whole day looking through the Internet—amazed at the images—and decided that they wanted to visit the beautiful, lively planet with its many varied species. But then there was the question— how would they get there?

Oasis pulled out her spaceship design and waved it around above her.

"Don't you remember this?" she said impatiently. Her father had an ashamed expression for a moment, but then brightened up a little.

"I forgot about it, but the good thing is we don't have to start from scratch. Now let's get to work," he said, pushing up his glasses with a determined air about him.

They got the tools and materials from the storage room built right next to the lab and began putting everything together. It took them about half an earth-year to finish the spaceship, and another half-year to work out the bugs in the system. During that time, the taunts of her classmates mattered less and less to Oasis, and the more she ignored them, the more they left her alone. She still did not belong, however, and from time to time, after a long afternoon of homework and helping her father build the ship, sadness crept into her mind. But she never let it stay.

Finally, the spaceship stood before them, in all its glory. Oasis wiped away tears of joy. She was going to be one of the first Europans to go to another planet. Her father was already climbing into the cockpit, which didn't leave Oasis much time to pride herself on her accomplishments. He started the engine as Oasis got into the passenger's seat and the ceiling opened up so the ship could fly out of the lab.

The ship rushed through the murky waters and escaped through a gap in the icy surface of the planet. They marveled at the weightlessness as they escaped the atmosphere. Jupiter pulled the ship toward it with its gravity, though, and they struggled to escape it. The mass of the giant world snatched at them in greedy desperation, as if unwilling to share its lifeforms with the rest of the universe, but Turbo manipulated the controls with a nearly supernatural agility, and the pair finally escaped the gravity well.

Oasis turned to peer out of the rear window. Europa floated near Jupiter, looking small, cold and cracked, as if it already missed her and her father. She knew she would miss her home too, but she was excited about visiting Earth as well. And somehow, out here in the blackness of the void, she felt she had found her place, her purpose. She was an explorer, and she would never be content with any home beside the vast gulf between the stars.

"Goodbye to all that, I guess," she sighed softly and turned forward again. Her father broke his concentrated stare for a moment to flick his eyes toward her and smile broadly. In that moment, in that look of joy, Oasis understood that even as an explorer, she would never be alone. There would be fellow travelers, always.

Charlene Bowles

THE STRANGE CASE OF HUGO ROSE

Dr. Kevin King walked the narrow halls of Verrilville Sanitarium, a folder that read *Hugo Rose* in one hand and a guard named James Barker to his left. The outstretched hands of the insane reached through the small windows set at eye levels in each door. They screamed outrageous claims of celebrity, murder, obscenities, and nonsense. Officer Barker bashed his night stick against the doors of the inmates as he walked by.

"Shut up!" he shouted. "Sorry about them, Doc, but you're the one who wanted to talk to this freak."

Dr. King smiled. "An apology is unnecessary, Officer Barker."

Barker patted King on the shoulder. "Ah, hell, Doc. Call me Jim; everyone does."

Dr. King rubbed his shoulder as if annoyed.

The cries of the insane grew distant as they approached the end of the long, narrow, hall. An eerie silence came from the door at the end. A faded sign that read *H. Rose* had collected a nice coat of dust, making the name nearly illegible. "This is his room," said Officer Brooks. "I'll be right outside. Give a holler if you need anything." He unlocked the rusty door.

"That won't be necessary Jim." Dr. King said reassuringly. "I'm sure I'll be fine."

Beneath the dull light of an overhead lamp sat one Hugo Rose. Convicted murderer. A body count that surpassed that of any known serial killer in the annals of history. A confirmed body count of 257 people. His long hair was streaked with gray. His head rested on his forearms, as if he were sleeping.

"Hugo Rose?" presumed Dr. King.

Rose sighed deeply. "If I told you I was someone else, would you kindly leave?"

Dr. King did not respond. He simply nodded to himself and sat across from Hugo Rose. "My name is Dr. Kevin King," he said with a hint of pride. "I'm here to evaluate you and determine whether or not you can be transferred from solitary confinement to general population."

Hugo chuckled at the words pouring from Dr. King's mouth.

"Do you understand what I am telling you, Mr. Rose?"

Hugo looked up at Dr. King. His dark eyes were blood-shot as though he'd been weeping. "How do I make you go away?"

"You talk to me."

Hugo looked at the door and then at Dr. King. "Go to hell, Doc." He put his head back down.

"Fine. I've got nothing but time."

At this, Hugo Rose laughed. "No. *I've* got nothing but time. You have about ten more years left to you, buddy. If you're lucky."

Dr. King sat up and looked Hugo Rose in the eye. "You don't frighten me, and you can't intimidate me."

Rose stiffened and returned the gaze. "What exactly is it that you want from me?"

"Just to talk."

Hugo Rose smiled. "I do nothing for nothing, Doc."

Dr. King reached into his coat pocket and pulled out a deck of cards and a pack of cigarettes. He placed them in front of Hugo.

"Now we're talking." The prisoner reached out and pushed the cigarettes aside. He pulled the cards from the deck and began to shuffle. His hands moved with the cards like waves on sand. The cards were almost a part of him.

"You're very good at that."

"Some used to say I was the best."

"Let's talk about that, shall we?"

Hugo held the deck out in front of him. "Pick a card." he beckoned. Dr. King gave him a puzzled look. "My cards. My game. My rules."

"What's the game?" asked Dr. King.

"High card draw. If you get a higher card than me, I get to ask you a question. You get the high card, you get to ask me a question. Deal?"

King didn't think it was a fair or logical deal to make, but Rose would not cooperate otherwise. He drew a card. "Deal."

The prisoner smiled and let out an excited laugh. "Oh this should be fun." He shuffled the deck, and pulled out a card. "The king of hearts. Difficult to top, Doc."

King turned his card. "The ace of clubs beats it."

Hugo smiled and set down the deck. "Okay, Doc. Shoot."

The doctor sat back placing his own card face down. "Why murder? What drove you to kill so many people?"

As quickly as the smile had arisen on Hugo's face, it was gone. "What do you know about Death, Doc?"

The question puzzled Dr. King. "Death is a natural part of life..."

"No, no, no." Hugo interrupted. "I didn't ask what your philosophies on death were. I asked what you know about *him*."

Dr. King focused hard on the way Hugo made mention of death. "Him?"

Hugo opened his eyes wide in mock surprise. "Oops. He's crazy again." He began to cackle at a joke that only he seemed to get.

"How is that funny, Hugo?"

"Because you already assume that I'm completely in-sane. You think that I rationalize homicide by giving something as 'natural' as death not only a face, but also a gender. You've already deemed me crazy."

Dr. King was astounded by the man's perceptiveness. Hugo was right He already felt in his mind that Hugo Rose was completely insane.

Hugo sat back. "We're through here. You can go."

Dr. King raised his hand in gesture of forbearance. "No. Tell me more, Hugo. I want to know everything about you. How long have you seen the face of Death?"

Hugo chuckled. "You're patronizing me."

"I am not. I'm honestly curious."

Hugo stared into Dr. King's eyes for a moment as if trying to understand his curiosity. "I think it would be best to start from the beginning, Doctor..."

"Perfect. Where did it all begin for you?"

"You wouldn't believe a word of what I'd tell you."

"According to you, I already think you're crazy. So what would it matter if you were to tell me that you threw the moon into the sky?"

Hugo guffawed. "Don't be ridiculous, Dr. King." His attention seemed to drift momentarily, and then he intoned, almost solemnly, "I died once, in the year 1349..."

"The Black Plague?"

"No. I lived in the Northern parts of Europe. The Plague was an eastern disease."

"Go on."

"In Northern Europe, I was a once a great magician. And a gambler extraordinaire. My gambling habits seemed sure to be the death of me, but my victories were as impressive as my magic." Hugo held up a card, and with the flick of his wrist, changed its face.

The doctor whistled. "Impressive."

"I know."

"So... how did you die?"

Hugo began to shuffle the cards. "I cheated one too many times at a game I was already good at. And one day I cheated a man who didn't take to kindly to losing. His name escapes me, but his knife certainly didn't." Hugo pulled up his shirt to reveal a mass of scars across his body. He pointed to one over his heart. "He drove what could have easily been a nine-inch blade into my heart"

Dr. King stopped him. "A nine-inch blade in your heart would have instantly killed you."

"Oh, I'm sorry. Was my story boring you?" Hugo snapped.

"No. It's just not logical that..."

"Oh I understand. Perhaps another story would peak your interest? Would you like to hear the story of how I slaughtered several women in Whitechapel, London in 1888? Or perhaps the time I made love to the woman who drove the Marquis de Sade to sadism? Or maybe..."

"Hugo." Dr. King looked apologetic and chagrined. "I'm sorry. I didn't mean to come off as condescending."

Hugo grabbed the cigarettes. "Well, you did. Now, do you want to hear this story or not?"

The prisoner put a cigarette to his mouth. Dr. King lit it. Hugo exhaled a cloud of smoke and sighed deeply. "I don't take kindly to being called a liar. I'm a great many things, Doc. A bastard. A fiend. A murderer. Hell, a cheater. But a liar?" He shook his head.

"My apologies Hugo. I promise not to interrupt you again."

"The pain wasn't as bad as you might imagine. But the darkness afterwards." Hugo shivered. "I lost consciousness, or so I thought. I hit the ground with a knife in my chest. The last thing I remember was screaming. In what felt like a blink," he snapped his fingers, making Dr. King jolt, "I opened my eyes. The bar patrons were gone. The seats were empty. I stood up, thinking that I was okay, but it was different. Everything was different. Everything was gray. And cold. God, it was so cold. There was a man sitting at the table I had been at moments before. He was occupying the seat the guy who stabbed me had used. He had on an old black coat, and his eyes were black. Like shadows in the sunlight, his eyes were so black. I didn't have to ask. I knew exactly who he was." Hugo recalled...

His voice trembles with fear. "Please." His breath clouds his face. "Don't take me. I'm not ready to go."

The man whom Hugo Rose calls 'Death' speaks in a low and calm voice. "Desire is for those who remain Earth bound. The dead will eternally desire life, as fish eternally desire water. Desire is obsolete where we are going."

Hugo Rose falls to his knees. "Please, I beg you. Not me. I can't be dead."

Death's face only moves when he speaks, no hints of emotion. "Save your fear for your maker. I'm simply the chauffer to your eternity."

Hugo stands up. "What if I refuse to go?"

Death rises and almost towers over Hugo. "A fool laughs in the face of Death. There is no word, adequate to describe a man foolish enough to challenge it."

Hugo looks into the abyss that is the eyes of Death. "Are you a gambling man?" he asks.

"What are the stipulations?" asks Death.

Hugo reaches for the deck of cards that rests on the table. He begins to shuffle them. "High card draw. If I pull a higher card than you, you let me live."

"And if I pull the higher card?" asks Death.

"I'll go quietly."

With this, Death extends his long hand to Hugo who reaches back out to him. Death clasps his cold hand around Hugo's, and smiles a smile that has haunted the dreams of Hugo Rose ever since.

"Deal," says Death.

Hugo shuffles the cards and spreads them out. Death reaches out and pulls his card. It is now Hugo's turn. He thumbs through the cards, searching for the ace of spades that he has marked. He finds it. He slowly pulls the card as if expecting Death to call his cheat, like the man who stabbed him in the chest what seems an eternity ago. Death places his card face up on the table. The king of hearts. Hugo then sets his down beside it. The ace of spades. Death stares at Hugo's card.

"A deal's a deal. right?" says Hugo.

"I suppose it is," Death replies. He extends his hand back out to Hugo. Hugo clasps it. Death holds on tightly. Hugo tries nervously to pull away from Death, as that same sinister smile comes back across his face.

"No!!" Hugo cries out. "You said you'd let me live!"

Death draws Hugo close to him. "And I shall. Hugo Rose, you will only live to regret this."

The black apparition lets the magician go. He falls to the floor, trembling in fear.

"He let you live?" asked Dr. King.

"It seemed so at first. But he never came back."

"What do you mean?"

"I thought at first that Death let me live a while longer, but after 20 years, I hadn't aged. I married, I had children, and I had to watch them grow old and die." There was a pain in Hugo's voice. "Don't you understand? He abandoned me."

King was dumbfounded. "I don't understand. Hugo, are you telling me that you're immortal?"

Hugo put the cigarette out on the floor. "That's exactly what I'm telling you! When I realized that Death would never come for me, I began to see him. Every time someone died anywhere near me, I could see Death taking them to their judgment. I watched him take my wives, my sons, my daughters, my friends, everything! I would scream to him, beg him, plead with him to take me with him. To take me to my punishment. But this is it. This is my punishment. Immortality."

"I don't understand. How can immortality be a punishment?"

Hugo regarded the doctor with disgust, as if he'd been insulted. "Only a man who has never lived an entire lifetime would ask such a stupid question. Ever since I realized that death would not take me willingly, I have done everything in my power to gain his attention. You think that 257 dead people is a lot? I am a walking, talking holocaust! I have spilled the blood of *thousands* of people, just to have another opportunity to beg Death to take me. I have watched this world collectively destroy itself. We create and create, to simply tear each other apart. I have watched enemies become friends, and friends become enemies. I have watched the technological advancement of execution. I've seen humanity go from the guillotine to the nuclear bomb. I have witnessed young men kill each other for the idea of freedom. I have witnessed the mass suicides of blind followers of faith. I have watched those same faithful kill in the name of a god that has never spoken a single audible sentence to them. I have watched us destroy ourselves over a span of 800 years, and the only difference between now and then is that we slaughter each other in the comfort of central air conditioning. In the 800 years that I have lived on this green Earth, the only thing that I still fear is tomorrow. Because only God knows how we'll destroy one another tomorrow."

Dr. King stood up. "This interview is over." He began to gather his things.

"Have I been deemed sane, Dr. King?" Hugo asked sarcastically. "Will I be given access to a more general population?"

Dr. King knocked on the door and peered out the small window. "Officer Barker?" he called out. There was no response.

"I'm talking to you, Dr. King." Hugo's voice was menacing. Standing with deliberate slowness, he took a few steps toward his visitor.

Fear twittering within him, the psychologist looked back at the prisoner, in whose eyes strange passions roiled. Swallowing heavily, he found enough courage to pass judgment. "It is my opinion, Mr. Rose, that you are not competent enough to socialize with the general population of the sanitarium, and it will be my recommendation that you remain here for a duration of no less than one year before you are re-evaluated. Officer Barker, please open the door!"

Hugo Rose looked over Dr. King's shoulder out the window and gave a nervous chuckle. "That doesn't look like officer Barker to me," he said with ominous calm.

The psychologist turned to peer out the small square of reinforced glass. The long hallway that Dr. Kevin King had walked down what seemed an eternity ago began to go gray. King's breath misted as a sudden chill filtered through the door. A figure was walking toward Rose's cell from the opposite side of the narrow hall, his coat long and black, his eyes a dark abyss.

With unexpected fury, Hugo Rose's hands clasped tightly around King's throat. But strangely the doctor felt only the cold yet welcome embrace of a comforting hand as the screams of Hugo Rose faded along with his life.

"Take me!" Hugo Rose was shouting. "Please take me!"

Bobby Brown

LYING DOWN FOR POWER

Penawʉhtamʉ crossed into Sonora on the third day of his journey, dust enshrouding him in a ghostly pall. The council of his nʉmʉnakhani, the extended family group that had guided him to this, the cusp of manhood, had murmured gruff approvals at the choice of puhakatʉ: the Spanish horseman had taken the lives of many Apache before dying under their arrows, and the cave in which his Nʉmʉnʉʉ allies had left his body was surely burgeoning with power. With truth. With puha.

"What is more," his father Tosamʉa had intoned through a haze of tobacco smoke, "your mother was of the Spaniards' bastard race. Fitting you should lie down for power in such a place."

If there had been any reproach in the observation, no one seemed to mark it, and Penawʉhtamʉ kept to himself the strange vertiginous feelings that thoughts of his mother, dead for nearly six years, sent swirling through his gut. He knew himself to be nʉmʉ, a true person, a member of that race the Spanish had disparagingly called "Comanche," culling that name from the insulting invective of its enemies. Nonetheless, he could not escape the irony of his mother's identity, even given the rising numbers of half-breeds within this, the southernmost division of Nʉmʉnʉʉ, called Orientales by the Mexicans. Gertrudis Vallejo de Becerra, the woman who had given birth to Penawʉhtamʉ some fourteen summers previous, along with her five-year-old daughter, Augustina Becerra Vallejo, had been taken by Penawʉhtamʉ's fathers while en route to Mexico City from San Antonio de Béxar. Until he had moved into his own dwelling three years ago, Gertrudis (Puhihwi wa'ihpʉ, her new people named her) had been intimately involved in his upbringing, and she had not permitted him to ignore the Spanish side of his ancestry. Acutely aware of his heritage, Penawʉhtamʉ felt at times torn between a desire to destroy mejicano warriors and a need to learn more about them: this vision quest promised to strike a balance between the conflicting sides of his soul.

Closing his mind to the grating dust, Penawʉhtamʉ recalled the words of Wesikitʉ, the band's most respected puhakatʉ—it was him the men and women called upon when in need of truly transformational or healing puha—as the old shaman had bathed him in the waters of the Pecos River: "A man must find his own truth, his own power. You want the power of the mejicano warrior; who can say what spirit will grant it to you? Be cautious, be prepared for a difficult vision. If you follow the traditions, if you honor the spirits as I have instructed you, then one of them will deign to favor you. Then you will yourself become a puhakatʉ, able to join your fathers and uncles and the other warriors on raids. Honor will accrue to you, and you may grow to become a *tekwʉniwapi*, leading forays yourself; perhaps you will garner as much puha as I, or indeed you may win enough respect to become a *paraibo*, like your grandfather, mighty leader of our band for so many years now."

Wesikitʉ had motioned Penawʉhtamʉ from the water, and the boy had solemnly donned his breechclout and moccasins. Once the shaman's wife had braided Penawʉhtamʉ's hair—dark brown rimed with reddish-gold—the old man had asked him ritualistically for the four sacred objects:

"Do you have your buffalo robe, my brother?"

"Yes, I do." The woman draped it over his shoulders.

"Do you have your pipe at the ready?"

Penawʉhtamʉ lifted it in the midday light. "Yes, I do."

"Do you have tobacco which to smoke?"

"Yes, I do." The woman hung the pouch round his neck.

"Do you have your flint with which to light it?"

He clutched it in his other hand, held it above his agitated heart. "Yes, I do."

The band's shaman took up a smoldering stick and waved its smoke upward and in the four cardinal directions. He gestured at the boy to face the sun, already climbing the eastern sky, and he muttered a prayer: "Great Father, you who abide beyond the sun, watch over this nʉmʉ as he undertakes a quest farther than any before. Guide him to the place where his spirit awaits him; remind him constantly of his duties and rites; bring him close to the truth that is his alone."

The old man turned his eyes upon Penawʉhtamʉ. "Many days stand between you and the lands the Mexicans have usurped from the buffalo: never have I known a boy to travel so far in search of puha. You are not permitted to eat, however, no matter the distance, and you must still stop only four times to smoke and pray. Once you have arrived at the cave you seek, you know what you must do."

Penawʉhtamʉ had begun walking roughly southward. He estimated at the beginning that it would take him some three days and nights to reach the Río Bravo, but he had not fully appreciated what physical stress such a journey would entail: when he paused to sit for smoke and prayer after the first full day of walking, he felt he would not be able to stand again. Dropping a pinch of tobacco on the ground, he blew smoke toward the eastern sky: "Father, stir the spirits of the air, have them make my journey easier, lessen your fire upon my head." He sucked on the pipe again, his lack of food increasing the narcotic effect of the tobacco, making his head swim. He puffed at the ground: "Mother Earth, make yourself soft beneath my feet; encourage the spirits of rock and sand to grip more firmly the heat of the day so the night will be warmer; put springs in my path before I reach the great river; let desert flowers refresh my air." Finally, he looked up at where Mother Moon had not quite dipped below the horizon, her silver form going transparent white beneath the glare of Father Sun. "Night-mother, shine for your son. Keep me from the darkness in which the lost souls wander. Illumine my heart."

And closing his eyes, head swimming, he had risen to his feet and begun to walk once more. The third morning of his journey, after he said his second prayer, it took Penawᵾhtamᵾ nearly a half hour to crawl to a large boulder and hoist himself up. It appeared to him on that third day that he was on the verge of the spirit world. He seemed to perceive wavering forms all about him; once, he even heard his mother chanting low in Spanish: *duérmete mi niño, duérmeteme ya...*

By the time he reached the Río Bravo, Penawᵾhtamᵾ no longer felt hunger or pain: he had passed beyond those quotidian worries now. In his buffalo robe, he wrapped up his moccasins, breechclout, tobacco and pipe. Holding the bundle upon his head, he plunged into the cold waters of the great river and swam across, not frightened by the lulling pull of the current nor the ancient spirit that murmured for him to let himself sink to join her in the watery depths, calling to him in Spanish, naming him her son. It was twilight when he reached the far shore, and he had to stop, had to smoke and say his third prayer.

He woke with a start when the pipe spilled from his hand, sending its burning contents onto his legs. He hauled himself to his feet, no longer feeling himself a being of flesh but of pure spirit. The cave was only a half-day's journey southwest, but Penawᵾhtamᵾ could have traveled another ten days: he had transcended himself.

White with the desert's grainy dust, he made the cave at sunrise. Its yawning aperture faced south, a propitious sign as sitting before it permitted him a clear view of both east and west. The boy collapsed a bowshot's distance from the cave, pulling out his tobacco, stuffing the pipe with shaking hands, and lighting it finally after many failed attempts. He mumbled his prayers, feeling consciousness slip alarmingly away, and he snuffed the pipe's contents on the sand, only barely able to stretch his legs westward and cover himself completely with the buffalo robe before hurtling into the chasm of sleep that awaited him. It was likely he would sleep all day and through the night, and even as his mind shut down, he instinctively shrouded his face against the eventual darkness of night. He was alone in the desert, and in danger of being killed: death in the dark could doom his spirit to wander forever in the gloom, unable to reach the land beyond the sun where all was light and the hunt was eternal.

He awoke, parched and feverish, under the broiling sun of the following afternoon. The spirit world, which only a day ago had seemed to swirl about him, was nowhere to be perceived, its undulating forms obliterated by deep and dreamless sleep, by the sharp hunger that twisted his insides, and by the insistent ache of every muscle in his body. He drank deeply from his water skins, arranged his robe beneath him, and sat staring at the entrance to the cave. Taking out his pipe, he loaded it, struck his flints, and puffed smoke as he intoned his invocation: "Spirit that dwells in this place, that gave the mejicano his power, hear my prayer. Grant that which I desire, the secret of the man's power, and all my days I will honor you and sing your songs." Pausing to consider the possibility that the spirit might only speak Spanish, Penawuhtamu repeated his petition in the language his mother had taught him, a language used by his own people to communicate with Apaches and Kiowas: "Espíritu que aquí moras, que le distes al mejicano su *puja*, escucha mi rezar. Concédeme mi deseo, el secreto del poder de ese hombre, y toda mi vida te voy a honrar y voy a cantar tus canciones."

Then the waiting began. Penawuhtamu tried to keep his mind clear, but unbidden images and thoughts bubbled up from somewhere. Though he had been too young to actually remember that day, he experienced a vision of his half-sister

Augustina as she had slipped from his mother's lodge, leaving him to toddle ineffectively after her as she had made her escape. As he tried to focus on her features in his mind's eye, he could not recall them, but only saw his own face framed by her golden hair. He wondered whether she had made it back to the mejicanos at Béxar, or whether she'd found death or captivity before reaching her own people.

After a while, images began simply to stream through his mind; moving along the Pecos, following buffalo northward and southward, wrestling with friends, pre-adolescent sexual games. His horse, a beautiful *ohaesi* or yellow roan named Tatsinuupi, his best friend, awaiting him under the shaman's protection. In the desert stillness, he replayed scene after scene of his life, only moving to sip water, allowing the sacred sun to steep his being in its trying heat. No spirits spoke to him that day, and as dusk settled, his hunger having weakened him further than he'd ever thought possible, Penawʉhtamʉ pulled the buffalo robe over his head and slept dreamlessly.

The next morning he once again prayed, to the Father, the Mother, the Moon, the spirits that might be near; sitting cross-legged on the robe, he focused on the gravelly sand, honey peppered with glinting black. He stared unblinking at the desert till it seemed to flow like a lake, reflecting the sun's inscrutable face back up at it. Hunger, thirst, heat and nausea began to fade as the edges of the world bled away in a steadily encroaching sfumato. The sable noose of heat stroke reduced his field of vision to a distant oval in which he saw reenacted the great stories of his people, bracketed always at beginning and end by his grandmother's voice hoarsely murmuring *soobe'sʉkʉtsa' rʉa* and *subetʉ*. He saw the First Horse come up out of the desert, challenging the People to break them, swearing he and his band would be their companions forever if they could. Kawus was there before him, brave hero of ages past, stampeding the buffalo out of the enormous subterranean corral, disguised and aided by Brother Coyote. These legendary deeds were followed by the great history of recent times, mighty battles carried out by Ecueracapa, Esanatʉhka (known as "el Sordo") and Cordero, along with his fathers' own raids and coups. Thus the entire day played out, his people's lore dancing in shimmering mirages before his eyes, distracting him, shutting out the spirit voices that might open the way to power for him.

Penawʉhtamʉ was ravaged again that night by intense fever, and he heard beyond the thin protection of his buffalo robe the clattering of bones against rock, a dull groaning and shuffling; in an agonizing moment that pushed him to the limits of his courage, he felt something hard brush against his shoulder, leaving a cold sensation behind that sank fangs into his soul. He finally fell into a fitful, phantasm-filled sleep.

At daybreak, he resolved not to spend another night in that place. It occurred to him that there might be a way to reach the spirit of that place more directly. Shambling about on uncooperative legs, Penawʉhtamʉ ranged in a wide arc, his eyes hunting the dusty ground for the tell-tale pink flowers. After about an hour, his search was successful: he knelt beside the blue-green plant and pulled it up, tapering root and all. Back at the cave's entrance, he drank the remaining water in his skins and carefully removed the plant's mushroom-like headdress and said a prayer to the spirit of the area. Then, popping the peyote into his mouth, he walked into the dark mouth of the cave.

Inside, the air was quite a bit cooler. Penawʉhtamʉ stood silently, chewing on the acrid plant and allowing his eyes to adjust to the gloom. His stomach twisted in nausea, but he managed to swallow and keep the peyote down. Once his vision was clear, he could make out the skeleton of a man dressed in tattered black leaning against a boulder about ten paces from the entrance. Tarnished silver bangles on his worm-eaten clothing verified for the young man that this was indeed the mejicano, who had been a famous *jinete* or *charro*, spectacular horse riders second only to the Nʉmʉnʉʉ themselves. Near him were the worn remains of his saddle, several leather and cloth bags, and a large dusty mirror on the cave floor flawed by a complex moiré of cracks.

Penawʉhtamʉ dropped heavily to the ground. Time seemed to slow as he stared at the mejicano's skull, and from the deep black chasms of the dead man's eyeholes he felt a hypnotic calm stream into his body. His breathing gradually slowed, his pulse dropped below its normal rhythm.

After an interminable period of staring at the dusty mirror, Penawʉhtamʉ began to see smoke curling from the cracks, as if a fire had been kindled beneath it. Strengthening this impression, the mirror began to darken, and strange glints of phosphorescence seemed to eddy in its depths. But then the surface of the mirror bulged, rippling upward as if something *within* the mirror were pushing out, the way a person's hand might stretch the filmy membrane of a buffalo's stomach. Then it was as if the surface of the mirror tore, and an impossibly enormous black paw thrust itself into the air, bending and stretching forward to sink vicious ebony talons into the rocky dirt. A voice from somewhere within Penawʉhtamʉ urged him to draw his knife, to flee, to do something, but its words echoed faintly as if from far away, and his eyes remained, with the rest of him, firmly fixed in place. Another massive paw ripped through with an audible groaning, as if the very fabric of the world had been rent by its grappling claws. These two... forelegs of some dread beast tensed as if against some great weight, and with an agonizing howl that thrummed the rock of the cave and sent a shower of scree raining against Penawʉhtamʉ's head and back, an indescribably huge black puma erupted from the mirror, smoke curling from its rippling flesh as it snarled and shook itself.

Penawʉhtamʉ's mind desperately tried to fold in upon itself, to turn away from the horrid, steaming beast whose bright green eyes now focused upon the young Comanche;

there was no turning away, however, and gibbering internally, Penawuhtamu awaited his doom. The ears of the puma, twitching this way and that, nearly scraped the cave's high dome, and its tail slapped angrily against the farthest wall, knocking loose shiny cascades of minerals. The rocky earth recoiled against the touch of three of its deadly paws, causing them to sink deep in the ground; the fourth appeared trapped within the mirror, which was now as black and smoky as an awakening fumarole.

Leaning its great head down to with arm's reach of the catatonic boy, the puma opened unspeakable, slavering jaws to reveal teeth the length of a man's leg and a gullet that glistened darkly with ominous implications. A rumbling growl was born in the depths of this black mountain, building toward a crescendo as Penawuhtamu could only dig his fingers into the abrasive soil and await his doom. But the growl, unexpectedly, became a voice: a voice like the fulminating call of the Thunderbird, but speaking in words Penawuhtamu could understand. The puma was addressing him in Spanish, antiquated and replete with difficult words, but intelligible nonetheless.

Have I your attention, boy?

The voice was all around him, echoing in the air, trembling in the ground, whispering in the very depths of his soul. He could not but answer it.

"*Sí, poderoso.*"

Powerful one.   Yes, that is apt.   It is good that you understand that I am powerful.   It is also good that you have not run.   I have awaited someone like you for centuries, Penawuhtamu.

"I came to await power, Lord."

And power you shall have.   More, mayhap, than you had hoped.   More than you may eventually desire.   First, however, let me assume a less theatrical form.

The great puma began to shudder, its limbs convulsing as though palsied or epileptic. Then, with heaving and pulsing, its flesh began to shrink and run together, gradually taking on another form; still imposing, the spirit now appeared to be a giant of a man, a forearm's length taller than the tallest man Penawᵾhtamᵾ had ever seen, with the skin of the black puma draped around him like a robe, its head hooding him and enfolding his handsome pale face in shadows. Behind his head, inexplicably floating in space, smoked a black mirror, made, in Penawᵾhtamᵾ's estimation, from obsidian. The young man was reminded for a moment of the Catholic icons his people came upon during raids, the saints with their circles of light. Except this was a circle of darkness, absolute and purest night. The apparition wore a grey tunic beneath the robe, decorated with black and grey feathers from, Penawᵾhtamᵾ noted, crows and ravens and vultures. His right foot was shod in a sandal, but his left leg tapered to bare bone just above the ankle, and the skeletal left foot appeared to be caught within the slightly convex surface of the mirror that still smoldered on the cave floor.

Jaguar.

"Pardon?"

Not puma. It is called a jaguar. But that is not important. I am named Tezcatlipoca, my son. Does that name not stir something within you, some trace of racial memory? No? It does not matter. However, it is of the essence that you understand something: I am no simple earth spirit come to give you a weak spell for healing wounds or some incantation for imbuing limbs with battle might. I am the master of death. I am everywhere. I effect change, pull down the old ways in favor of stronger ones, destroy the weak. I existed before this world's beginning, and I shall be here at its end. And I have a special purpose for you and for your people. A special destiny. For you to understand, I must tell you a story. I shall simplify it so you can more readily understand its point.

The specter drew its hands out from beneath the puma... the *jaguar* robe. In its right was gripped a long, curved obsidian knife with which it touched his forehead. As the cold stone cut into his flesh, a bright light exploded in his mind. The brightness dimmed slightly, and he saw, as in a vision, Tezcatlipoca at the side of a double, identical to the dark apparition except for the gaiety of his multi-colored and heavily feathered garments.

I have a brother, a simpering coward whom you will despise if you meet him. Without consulting with me, he, once we had seen to the emergence of mankind upon the face of the world, drew a special group into a paradise that their descendants would call Aztlán. *An island in the midst of incredibly clear water, white stone buildings scraping at the sky, proud people tilling the earth.* **His hope was to keep me from them, but that is beyond his power and duty. Rather than maintain them trapped and weak in that soft island of white, I convinced most of them to abandon the insipid paradise for a future replete with adventure and expansion and conquest, with struggle and glory, with victory and prize-winning.** *Caves on the island. A great exodus through darkness, the sound of the ocean above them, emergence into a twilight land.* **And they spread, moving out and gradually southward. Every place they stopped, they conquered and controlled.** *Battles, blood; songs and dancing. Slow but steady movement south.*

But my brother, as is his wont, slowly interfered, not letting me see him, but working through intermediaries. Eventually he split a group off while I drove the rest ever downward. Mine swept over what is now called Mexico, named for their descendants, the Mexica; his stayed put, and became, among others, the group called Shoshone by the Whites. *Quickly alternating visions of mighty warriors, their towering edifices running with blood, and groups* *of hunters on foot, bringing down buffalo as the Father had from the beginning ordained they do.* **Of course, he was not content to leave the Aztecs, the former citizens of Aztlán, to carry out the destiny they had chosen; he interfered with them as he had done before in the same area centuries before. At first he kept my followers from gaining victory; he whittled down their numbers by various ruses, deceived them into becoming enslaved to the tribes of the deep South where the jungle begins.**

I gave them a ruler, a son I fashioned. Huitzi-lopochtli, who led the Mexica to a great lake in the midst of which they were to build a mighty city. And they reestablished their superiority and ruled over their former masters. But my brother would not conscience this, and he slowly interfered again. The Mexica and their conquered people became weak and prepared to abandon their place as masters of this part of the world.

So I brought the Whites. *Horses, metal, guns flashing in the sunlight. Millions dead by disease and war. Catholic priests, the Mexica and their subjects kneeling for communion.* **But, my young Comanche warrior, it was not for the destruction of Mexico that I brought the Whites. I had not forgotten those of you whom my brother had led astray. I came to you from time to time, and I saw, at the same time that I realized the Mexica were flawed and weak, unable to rule, that you were a mighty and noble people. Yes, you. From the Shoshone you drew yourself erect under the awesome sun. The N̶u̶m̶u̶n̶u̶u̶. For you I brought the Whites, so you would make a pact with their horses, learn to merge with them, create a new warrior race, a symbiosis of man and beast, fierce enough to take the place of the Mexica and impose a very different sort of Aztlán on all this land.**

Penawᵾhtamᵾ's mind balked at the images of himself astride a red mustang, leading all the divisions of his people in an enormous army against the Mexican and American forces. *Impossible.*

Naught is impossible. I intend you, child, to be my spokesperson to your people. And I shall give you the tools you require, the help you need. Some things I shall give you now, others will be provided as you require them.

Here are my gifts. First, the smoking mirror.

The gigantic figure reached behind its head and seized the black obsidian circle. As Tezcatlipoca brought his arm down, the mirror began to shrink till, when placed in Penawᵾhtamᵾ's outstretched hand, warm and heavy, it only just extended past his fingertips. **This you shall place in the center of your shield. It is your *puhahante*, the symbol of your principal power and truth... death. After you have called up its might, your enemies will fall before you when they see themselves within its unfathomable circuit. Secondly, I bequeath you my knife. Affix it to the end of your spear once you have proven yourself a warrior in your people's eyes. It will slash through metal, flesh and bone effortlessly once you have invoked its power. To do so, to conjure the puha of my obsidian, this is the chant you shall declaim:**

> **Lápidas sables que sois mi pujanza**
> **Sed la faringe de toda venganza**
> **Orco abridles a mis enemigos**
> **Paulo con vos y así les maldigo**[1]

---

[1] Sable stones that are my power/ be ye the pharynx of all vengeance/ open ye Orcus to my enemies/ I confabulate through you and thus I do curse them

Penawɯhtamɯ shivered as invisible talons seemed to carve the words in his very soul. Nodding as if assured of the boy's memory, Tezcatlipoca flipped the knife over and handed it, hilt-first, to Penawɯhtamɯ. The blade fairly thrummed with barely contained destructive force. The youth, unable to clearly register the enormous power being given into his hands, stared numbly at the blade, as dark and incomprehensible as his own future. **Another gift I have already bestowed on you; when I touched you with that self-same blade, I opened your third eye, the eye of your soul. From now on, you will be able to see the unseen, to perceive the varied phantasmagoria which daily surround the host of blind humans, shaping their fates without their being aware. If aught of this spirit world seek to harm you, show it the blade or the mirror, which are my sigils. This gift of singular vision is necessary because it may come to pass that you will need to employ some of these creatures in my service. When that time comes, I shall provide you with the means to command them.**

Cautiously, Penawɯhtamɯ expressed a doubt. "What about your brother? Will I see his servants? Will they try to attack me?"

Tezcatlipoca smiled ruefully, a terrible smile that made the youth wished he'd never spoken. **He does not often carry out his attacks that way. No, he trusts in humans to make choices that favor him, to fight in his service and risk their lives alone without his help. You need only be wary of men and women with the light glowing at the center of their foreheads. They too can see, and they will know you for my servant at first glance.**

And for the moment, that is all the knowledge you require. Go back to your people now. Become a warrior. Rise through the ranks. Do not shirk your duty as a man. And when again you feel the

need to conjure me face to face, look instead for the green-eyed witch in Saltillo.

Like cold water to the face, Penawᵾhtamᵾ suddenly felt the thrall of peyote and panic yanked away, and he stood on wobbly coltish legs. Tezcatlipoca, shrinking toward the mirror, regarded him oddly for a second. **Penawᵾhtamᵾ.** **"Honey braids." Well, to mark you for your people, I shall now eat the honey from your soul and from your braids. You are black as night now. Naught of sweetness in you, ever again. Take the bundles of the Mexican horseman. Wear his chaps. You are my *charro*, boy.**

The spirit was smaller than the youth now, and its eyes twinkled mischievously. **And so you cannot disregard what I say as the urgings of some random spirit, regard me, Charro. Regard me well, Wolf-brother and trickster that I am!**

And before him, black-flecked sandy hide bristling in fury, stood Coyote, the ancient ambiguous god, bane and blessing of the Nᵾmᵾnᵾᵾ. With a growl, the god spoke in the People's tongue: *Ke yaketᵾ. Ke hina supana'iitᵾ. Charro ᵾnᵾ nahniahkatu'i. Tukanihumi'arᵾ ma'. Haa, wihpu tai nᵾhkaru'ika. Oha'ahnakatu me ᵾmi niikwiiyu.*[2] Then, with a final sucking sound, Tezcatlipoca/Coyote disappeared into the cracked mirror. The youth walked over to it and peered at his image, kaleidoscoped by the webbed surface; his hair was totally black, all trace of his mother's reddish-blonde eaten away. In the center of his forehead glowed a sinister glyph that he could not hide even by putting his hand over it. *I'm not seeing it with my eyes, but with my new eye.* Turning away, he pulled open the drawstrings of the mejicano's leathern satchel. Inside, wrapped carefully in oilcloth, were the black vestments of an expert

---

[2] Don't fear. You know nothing. You will be called Charro. It will be dark soon. Yes, then we will all dance. Coyote has said this to you.

horseman. Discarding his breechclout, the young man who had once been known as Penawuhtamu donned the silver-bangled pants and broad-rimmed black hat of the charro, and understood why this was his adult name, given him by his protector spirit. *El Charro.*

He emerged into the dusk and quickly found a deer, which he dispatched with a furrowed arrow and spitted, his stomach clenching and cramping at the smell as it crackled above the flames. Tomorrow he would head northward to present himself as a man to his tribe. But he was more than a man now, and he was hesitant to reveal to his group the true nature of his puha's source. Old Coyote, a spirit protector? He had no idea how his people would react to such news, or whether they would even believe him. No. Puma had taken pity on him and shown him the way to his personal truth. That half-truth was sufficient for now. His people's lore demonstrated an incontrovertible truth: Coyote was unreliable and unpredictable; his words never wholly trustworthy, his behavior inscrutable. If Tezcatlipoca truly was that ancient brother of Wolf, then his gifts would have hidden repercussions, and the power he gave would effect changes in the world that its user never intended.

But the allure of the power was too great for el Charro to refuse. For now, he would simply be as cautious as he could, using the black tools for his own honor and that of the tribe. *When I sense deception in them,* he told himself again and again, *I'll abandon them.*

Convinced that he was capable of imposing his will on this power, el Charro ate in silence, his third eye roving over the clattering black forms that gathered around him in the gloaming.

In other layers of existence, Tezcatlipoca laughed.

David Bowles

IN-BETWEEN

A vast meadow filled with tiny sunflowers extended endlessly across the horizon. A special light filtered through the place, radiating a certain magic. Millions of emotions captivated me, sweeping like a tide wave through my being. I breathed in the freshest scent, admired the most delicate breeze brushing the meadow, and closed my eyes peacefully.

Every sound was clear: the wind, leaves swirling in the air, but most of all, the calm echoing against the infinite space.

I opened my eyes. My vision struggled to adjust to the heavenly place, blinded by the beauty.

After being immobile for long, I dared to take a step; it was light and required no effort. Every body part seemed to be in tune. It was all too easy here.

Finally, after the enchantment and glory slowly wore off, I grasped some part of reality.

I gazed at my surrounding in amazement, wondering how on Earth I landed on this place. I could not recall anything of what had happened. A thick veil of confusion clouded my mind.

The question pounded inside my head for several more minutes.

Then a new air came to the place. The atmosphere had changed. I sensed that my senses were keener here.

He was coming closer to me. *Who* was not the question at the moment; I was concentrating on how close *he* was to me.

I turned around in a sudden movement.

There was light radiating from him. He had clear ocean eyes and honey hair.

For a while, I only stared back, not shocked or amazed; instead, emotionless. "Am I dreaming?" I whispered as if the place were formed of delicate glass capable of breaking with mere noise.

He looked at me and his eyes penetrated into the depths of my body, my soul. I already felt too vulnerable and exposed in front of him.

"No." He spoke very clearly. Effortlessly.

"Where am I?" I maintained my soft gentle tone.

He watched me with his intense eyes.

"You're in-between." He said this as if it was the clearest thing in the world.

The serenity of my surroundings engulfed me, bathing me, not allowing me to fret over his words. I closed my eyes momentarily, hoping to take in the entire place in a single gulp of breath. I opened my eyes and remembered him.

"I don't understand."

He was calm and poised. It felt like we had a million years for a simple conversation. Nothing felt rushed in here. Not much mattered here either.

"You're between your life and death," he clarified.

I expected a big hit from reality, a sudden ruthless awakening to his words. But nothing. I remained calm.

"I still do not understand."

He hardly appeared frustrated by lack of recognition. He waited patiently.

A gentle breeze swayed the sunflowers beneath us. It rocked the place and the wind almost took on a lullaby. I thought I could recall the particular tune but the memory was too distant. Too deeply buried somewhere.

"You're in a coma."

I closed my eyes, waiting. I had no particular idea of what to remember but I stood still.

"Do you remember?" he asked.

I shook my head, still immersed in the tranquility of the darkness.

"It'll come to you."

My eyes adjusted to the darkness, not bothered at all. I inhaled and exhaled carefully the fresh air, as if it were essential I memorize the aroma.

I fell in deeper. If I paid close attention, I thought I could hear faint voices calling out to me. *Jamie...Jamie...baby...open your eyes...*

They sounded so upset. I wanted to tell them that Jamie was going to be okay. I voiced it silently, but it appeared they didn't hear me.

"Who were they?" I asked him, looking at him.

"Your family."

My family.

I had vague traces of memories about them. The flashes of recognition darted past me too swiftly.

Then, I started remembering. I remembered the speeding Mustang hit me, sending me into an abyss. I hit my head against a rock. Afterwards, I only saw black.

My eyes gradually reopened.

"What do I do?"

"You can go back with them or keep going. If you keep going, you cannot go back."

"Keep going to where?"

He had the faraway look to him again. "You can head to your death."

I breathed. "Does it hurt?"

"No."

"If I want to go back..."

"Then simply walk back." He paused. "It's up to you." He began to move away slowly, deeper into the marvelous surroundings, closer to the source of the beauty.

I gazed at the place around me, marveling at how I had never encountered anything of this nature or close to it. Every detail invited me, from the sunflowers to the clear skies. I felt no despair, anxiety, frustration or emotions. I felt fulfilled in a way I had never experienced before. The place offered a million things I could never have in another life, a million places to explore, a million breaths of fresh air, a million moments of peace.

Far away, I head their voices again. They seemed so distant. They were so pained, it tore my heart but I could not deny myself the eternal peace I had found myself.

I started heading in the direction he had gone. The other side. It was going to be much better than the life before. I was beyond ready to go with him. I wanted to be in the place where I could feel nothing but the breeze ruffling with my hair with its delicate touch, the wind whispering in my ear, the sunflowers dancing around me.

I heard their voices again. *Jamie...* They woke something in me. Something in me turned toward them.

I stopped dead in my tracks.

Then I began walking the other way.

Cindy Jáimez

DRUNK DRIVERS ARE DOGS

Drunk drivers are dogs! And that's an insult—to the dogs.

Whenever I'm driving, two of the things I loathe encountering on the road are stray dogs and drunk drivers, but for conflicting reasons.

I have heard of stories of inebriated driving and its consequences countless times, but each new case never fails to baffle me: a Venezuelan student, visiting the country for a short English-language study, all preppy and beautiful, until she was disfigured by a drunk-driving accident-with more than 60% of her body burned, all of her fingers amputated, and her hair, ears, nose, lips, left eyelid and much of her vision gone; a woman, hit by a 28 year-old drunk driver at a restaurant parking lot in the city of Weslaco—she went into a coma until life support was pulled just a few days after. I could go on and on with these heartbreaking, poignant stories. But keeping up with the tragedies becomes strenuous and frustrating as the victims themselves grow nameless and end up as cold statistics, the perpetrator and the crime forgotten over time.

Society has done much to try to curb these incidents. And though we hope that those who have access both to the wheel and, regrettably, alcohol at the same time would learn from these events that range from the shocking to the fatal, they don't. Just a few months back, a friend blogged about being hit by a drunk driver. Fortunately, luck was on her side since she "only" got a broken arm and bruises on her face and neck. I know this is little consolation, but it could have been worse. So, obviously, no one would want to bump into an intoxicated driver on the road. As for the strays, I do not fancy seeing them on my drive either, but for opposite reasons.

To say I love dogs is an understatement. Over the years, I have picked up a number of strays, keeping some of them myself, and getting some adopted by friends who I know will take good care of them. In fact, I have come close to conducting a background check on these friends just to make sure they're fit to take the dog home. So, it just strikes a nerve to run across an emaciated, bewildered, and frightened domesticated animal. To begin with, why do people breed, sell, and/or buy them if they cannot take care of them? As a result of their owners' lack of responsibility, the animals just end up on the streets or at the humane societies, which are generally understaffed, gravely underfunded, but overly populated by strays and unwanted animals of all shapes and sizes. Perhaps even worse, the abandoned pets could land in the hands of money-hungry, thrill-seeking individuals that engage in animal fights. What did these creatures do to us that they have to suffer such retribution? I don't want to sound preachy or to force my own ethics and standards on other people, but we should knock some sense into ourselves on this issue. We human beings can speak freely of our feelings and concerns with words so that even the slightest things that offend us are brought to light, discussed, and acted upon. But who speaks for these animals?

At this point, let me shoot straight with a "modest proposal" (move over, Jonathan Swift!). Every time we see a stray, let's pick it up and take care of it. Let us give it a good home, or find one for it if we cannot provide that shelter ourselves. Surely the world still has a lot of people with a big heart willing and able to take the animals in. As for the drunk drivers, we should pull them over, pull them out of their car, and let them walk on the street regardless of the distance to their destination. Why, how many of us ever cared how many miles each stray had to walk, without 'decent' food and water for days, before somebody with a bigger heart stops and rescues them? That is if somebody does. If not, we know what happens.

I have never heard of a stray dog "running over" someone and hurting or killing them, but this is obviously true of drunk drivers! So the next time we see both on the road—stray dogs and drunk drivers—let's swap them.

That way each one gets what they deserve.

Virgilio B. Valencia

WHAT HIDES IN THE CLOSET...

"Sissy!" the evil children would howl. "Fruit!" the enormous bullies would yell as they'd push me around. The remarks would come nonstop, like a stampede of terrified elephants. Derogatory insults like these accompany members of my community throughout our entire lives, but the years have taught me to cope and to ignore the comments. Children tend to pounce on the weak similarly to the way a lioness does the slowest gazelle in a herd. That which isn't deemed normal is frowned upon in a society where normality is essential for acceptance. Thankfully, along this difficult path I've met compassionate individuals who have taken upon themselves the task of making my circumstances slightly more bearable and a little less frightening. Being unusual is never easy: coping and learning to accept being "abnormal" can test a person on many levels. The results of these tests are seldom embellished with a fairytale ending.

Hardships have befallen all of us in our lifetimes, but the cherry on top of my ill-fortune-flavored ice cream makes things that much more unpredictable and unstable for me.

I'm gay.

"He's just waiting for the right girl to come along," my mom tells her sisters to explain my lack of a girlfriend for the past eighteen years. If only she truly knew me. If only I had the courage to tell her who I really am. The biggest fear I harbor isn't flunking out of college; not even failing a final compares to the terror of finally revealing myself to my parents and family. I'd rather confront a full-fledged parade of homophobes any day than to have to confront the ones I love with that unacceptable, irreconcilable, devastating and, possibly, heartbreaking truth.

Society doesn't make things easier for people like me. "Faggots," they whisper, just loudly enough as we walk by. "What they are goes against the word of God!" others bellow at the tops of their lungs. I'm not too familiar with the Bible, but I'm almost positive that the words "understanding," "love," and "compassion" are found somewhere in those age-worn verses. Ostracism is an unavoidable part of growing up; however, that universal feeling of not belonging only strengthens when someone realizes that what makes him unique is deemed repugnant by an extremely biased society.

The members of the Gay Community are as normal and human as anyone else, yet unfortunately people fail to recognize this, driven away by their immediate repulsion to our sexual preferences. We aren't some sort of alien species that harbors some sort of life-threatening, skin-devouring disease, but that is pretty much how we're treated.

Forget society for a moment. I couldn't care less about how I'm perceived by a narrow-minded society. I only care about what my parents think of me. But with my dad being a full-fledged homophobic and my mom exhibiting borderline homophobia, what they would think of me after this revelation wouldn't be that pretty. How do you confess to your mother and father that the thing which horrifies them the most is in their presence every single second of every single day? Imagine that your having a home depended upon your complete silence and the rejection of who you truly are. Furthermore, visualize losing your family because they fail to accept the way you were born. These are just a few of the dilemmas that keep me up at night while I still have a bed under their roof.

So I ask you, what hides in the closet? Could it be a vicious, man-eating monster intent on satisfying its ravaging hunger? Maybe it's replete with clothes, in many beautiful colors, neatly arranged? Or just maybe, the closet harbors fragile lives that are hanging on an even frailer thread. Lives that depend upon staying in the confines of a dark, desolate closet full of frightened individuals who are all carrying the same burden upon their tired shoulders as me, a burden which is slowly, but surely, seeping the will to live out of us.

That life of neglecting my individuality isn't for me; I've taken the first step outside that cold prison, and so far I've liked what I've seen.

Alfredo Ortiz

CHILD NUMBER FIVE

Being a ghost is much like being born in a family of seven and finding yourself child number five. At least when you're a ghost you have a purpose. It might not be the most honorable purpose, but you still can derive some slight satisfaction if you indulge in your job: scaring people. See, as a ghost you are chosen to haunt the living and make them worry about the afterlife by delivering fear to the human race. Fear of the dark, fear of being alone, fear of that moment when the sun goes down and night falls. But like a ghost that has no one to haunt, being child number five has no purpose. No real *place*.

You wander into a super market with your family, conscious that if you are not careful a little side track action will result in their leaving you. It's happened to me twice already: forgotten by a distraction of the more important siblings.

Let me explain. Parents have their child number one, the firstborn, their pride and joy, the person who will continue their legacy, the beginning of creation in the family. He will without a doubt be favored amongst all. Then there's the second born child, a companion to the first born, his best friend, someone he can play with, tell his secrets to, defend, be his sidekick; the two of them will never be bored.

After that comes the third child, and for a moment the parents think *that's it*: no more children. He will be the baby of the family, the spoiled one because three is a good number. Children number one and two now have a mission to take care of child number three, the baby. For a while that is true. But then "she" is born, the fourth child and of course she is treasured beyond belief because she is so far the only girl. The princess to this palace. The heir to the Queen. She is loved in a way none of the other kids will ever understand. She is now whom they fight to defend against anything that stands in her way. To protect against all that hurts her. She is beautiful. Daddy's little girl.

Then your parents decide to get drunk one night not use protection and *boom*: the fifth is born. Me. A mistake. An "unplanned child," one more to add to the statistics of unplanned children. Another paycheck from the government, as our neighbors would call it.

And while during that first year I might have thought, "Okay, maybe I wasn't planned, but heck: I am now the baby of the family, the one who will get all of the attention. This isn't going to be so bad!" But a few days later...my parents get pregnant again! As if five wasn't enough.

And they have twins! Numbers six and seven. And without a shadow of a doubt they are more valuable than the rest of us, for they are a rare breed. Twins! Soon I am forgotten. Lost in the translation of siblings and attention. Gone from the face of the earth. I do try to get a drop of my parents' attention by getting in trouble or faking sick, but it doesn't work; instead, they think I'm a rebel, and they isolate me even more. Woe is me. The lonely soldier without his war to fight. A cowboy without his outlaw to catch. Even worse, a superhero without his arch enemy.

Javier David González

SELF-RELIANCE: THE END OF THE CYCLE

Humans have always been infatuated with progress. It is within our desires to wish to grow. Expansion is the name of the game. Of course, it is the Game of Life that I speak of.

But progression always comes to an end. History shows that nature works in cycles. Due to these cycles, it is inevitable that we will stumble. We will fall and lie with the earth. We will be nothing more than soil and dust.

To survive these moments of decay, you must learn to rely on yourself. To be alone in your thoughts is to seek solidity within the liquid nature of humanity. Build a foundation on a rock and become a stylite. Trust yourself and trust God.

The support and respect of our peers is important to us. We want to feel accepted and important. We want to strive for a common ground. But this is impossible.

When the stars and the galaxies align and the cosmos has its way, the storms will destroy our precious possessions. Eventually the world will be in turmoil and heaps of cadavers will surround us. Each of us will be alone and afraid, yearning for our now useless technology.

What will you do then? After a few days the strongest will wither and die. As humans it is in our nature to rely on others. But the others will be gone.

All I know is that I will survive. I will defy decay.

How? Through the *Art of Self-Reliance.*

If you wish to join me, find me! If you wish to find me, find God. If you find God, you have a chance. If you have a chance, that is all you need.

When the world is desolate and is nothing but a wasteland, I will return to land.

From my isolation I will be revived. With my dedication, I will seek what is mine.

In my kingdom I will live alone with God. We will climb the mountains and reach the stars. My people will be equal. Their lives will be just.

We will seek salvation and form a new covenant with God. We will search for utopia and create a heaven on Earth.

The *Art of Self-Reliance* and the hidden truth of nature will prevail in the end. If you are worthy, I will see you on the other side.

Que vivan las personas de la muy noble, imperial y coronada Villa de Madrigal de las Altas Torres.

Tengo la sangre en mi cuerpo. La sangre del Señor.

Matthew Alexander Madrigal

UN CUENTO DE NAVIDAD

Siempre recuerdo las navidades en México con toda la familia. El 24 de diciembre era un día lleno de alegría y emociones. Los tamales, los regalos, las risas, y la unión familiar. Qué cosas más bonitas. No se pueden olvidar.

Recuerdo que pasaba la noche anterior del 24 de diciembre en casa de mis abuelos. Mi abuelita se levantaba muy temprano, y yo junto con ella, porque sabía que iría al molino a comprar la masa para hacer los tamales. Teníamos que hacer fila en una larga línea donde todas las señoras se juntaban y platicaban historias de las vidas de sus hijos y sus nietos. Me gustaba escuchar porque algunos eran mis compañeritos de la escuela.

Al regresar a la casa nos hacía a mi abuelito y a mí unas ricas y calientitas gorditas de masa rellenas de huevo con chile o frijoles para almorzar y así poder esperar hasta que salieran los tamales. Aún recuerdo ese olor a masa cociéndose. Es algo inolvidable.

Un poco más tarde, mis tías, sus esposos y mis primos empezaban a llegar y la casa entera se llenaba de alegría. Ya estando todos juntos empezaba la gran fiesta. Así es como recuerdo el día 24 de diciembre, como *una gran fiesta*.

Después, cada una de mis tías tenía una tarea diferente. Mi mamá se encargaba de preparar los chiles de color para los diferentes guisos, mi tía Juana preparaba el guiso de pollo, mi tía Chelo preparaba el de puerco y mi tía Lety preparaba los frijoles. Mi tía la más chica se encargaba de poner a remojar las hojas secas de elote para los tamales, y por supuesto mi abuelita, como la dueña de la casa y líder de la familia, preparaba la masa y le daba el punto bueno para que estuviera perfecta.

Mi parte favorita era cuando ya todo estaba listo para embarrar la masa en las hojas para terminar los tamales, porque era cuando abuelita dejaba que las nietas mayores ayudaran. Era muy divertido ayudar porque eso significaba que ya estaba grande y tenía edad de estar con todas mis tías. Las tías nos aconsejaban, bromeaban, y me contaban sus divertidas historias. Era una experiencia inigualable.

Al terminar, abuelita y otra de mis tías llenaban los tamales con los guisos y los acomodaban en la hoya tamalera y había que esperar unas cuantas horas.

Durante el resto del día jugábamos, platicábamos, y escuchábamos música. Durante la tarde no podíamos faltar a las posadas, y disfrutar de los ricos tamales con café o champurrado, un atole de masa con sabor a piloncillo. Para terminar el día y esperar la media noche, seguían los regalos, las sorpresas, los abrazos, y las risas. Estas son algunas cosas que recuerdo cuando escucho mencionar *las navidades*.

Olga Lidia Cervantes

NUESTRAS MANOS

Era amor, indiscutiblemente, el de la mano izquierda por la derecha. Cuando colgaban de los brazos por la calle, las manos se encadenaban con los dedos. Abrazados, mi mano izquierda con tu derecha, teníamos que sacarle la vuelta a todas las cosas que se nos atravesaban. El amor de nuestras manos surgió un caluroso día de Julio. Mientras nuestras almas rodaban en el pasto de la colina, nuestras manos se daban pequeños besos. Beso tras beso se fueron conquistando, y cuando llegó la luna, mi mano izquierda le dio a tu mano derecha una flor morada. La flor estaba colocada entre la trenza de los dedos de nuestras manos. Los pétalos acariciaban los lunares de la espalda de tu mano derecha. No había corrido el aire por el vientre de mi mano desde esa noche intensa del verano. Mi mano no ha mirado a la tuya desde ese día que tu mano le bailaba de lado a lado. Mi mano está deprimida y no quiere salir del bolsillo de mi pantalón. Sólo piensa en el arcoíris que el baile de tus dedos le dibujó en el espacio

Yaresy Salinas

POETRY

SELECTIONS

SOUTHTEXASTOWN

The amber security glow
Replaces the mesquite campfire
To blind the night expanse
Of galaxies and fast walkers
That used to entertain the range rider.
Rumbling thunder without lightning
Is a tornado deed without a thought
Being long on love, short on life.
Sounds are assembled
From a drunken pickup,
A gun barrel's bark,
Or perhaps the hum of the _OPLESS BA_.
The coyote still wails
In answer to such emergencies,
Now running along the Armco
And not the barbed-wire borders.
The tall tales are kept alive
In sales meetings and before the judge
Whose grandpa witnessed, squatting
Before biscuits and a crackling flame.
Idle boys look to spray paint and rock throwing,
Unaware of the joys of cow-tipping
And even the old-timers in barber chairs
Try to recollect the brush-country stars.

Richard D. Givens

MCALLEN MORNING

Sunrise in McAllen...
A brochure flutters along the curb
Behind the lone street sweeper
Making the only strip of moisture the day will see.
The colored pamphlet flashes photos of citrus,
Early landmarks, airlines at Miller Field,
Places to dine under a palmed paradise.

Rings of activity yawn with firing burners.
The waft of tortillas spread from the inner core
As pesos for migas are traded in serious Tex-Mex.
Pigeons flap from phone poles to browse the park.

The surrounding commercial district has not yet begun.
Managers and staff will magically appear at their desks
In an hour. Meanwhile, Mexican Yellowheads make noisy
Lime-green circles in an air race around the library.

Farther out, neighborhoods void themselves of children
        in cars;
A moment's stop at school, then on to work, wherever.
Through the windshield, receding orchards pass.
Four-wheeled concert halls blare Selena, Reba,
        Smashing Pumpkins.

At the outer ring, retirees in plaid shorts exit new homes
To fiddle in the garden, or to meet other pensioners for golf.
The driveways are white, the trees are small,
The early air is filled with saws and the smell of pine lumber.

Holding the rings together are streets and phone wires
But more importantly, places to meet and unite in ideas
Of interest to both languages and cultures;
At school, church, the museum, Luby's, El Posito, H.E.B.,
From North and South to McAllen; only a river divides.

Richard D. Givens

ERUDITE VALLEY

Late, gray, Río Grande winter drive -
The ending of citrus; the beginning of grain.
We pedagogs and poeticules ponder
The road and the ways of the unschooled.
Immigrants struggle at the edge of town
Picking stray produce and words that suit.
We laughed at the hand-held sign by the truck
That said in red, "SE VENDE GREYFRUT,"
Then knew the way. The message was plain.

Richard D. Givens

LOCAL TIME

Morning clouds awake over the sun's scale
While an oak leaf breeze scatters clicking sounds
Upon the sidewalk to my door.

The hazy-white chases the yellow moon west
To commence the daily baking of the house
Bordered by traffic and snooping dogs.

The radio is on as I dress and gulp coffee
Chattering the same news and weather
And the Supreme Court again ruled predictably.

There's no need to fetch a paper from the hedge
In a place where current events never age
And local time spends too much by loitering.

I watch the mockingbird from the back window
And try to interpret his jumping up and down
On the electric line while in determined song.

There will be three solicitations today
Two by phone for credit cards and insurance
One by door to send someone else's kid to camp.

I have learned to say 'no' with politeness and poise
And before long, the sameness of this day
Collapses into dusk from its own boredom.

Once again I find myself between radio and bed
Still contemplating this evening's sunset
Which occurred just as planned on local time.

Richard D. Givens

MOVING PICTURES

The white palm, raised high,
Slapped washboard ground
In a dusty thud,
Claiming the playground and the first four cars.

Abiding to the winds of time
Like a giant pushing up from the table,
It said "That's it. No more show.
Prepare the way for the flea market."

Dirt settled amid headlights and hoots
And revving for the race to the exit.
No more "do-wah-ditty, she-bop-do-wah"
From the indestructible pot-metal that rarely worked.

No more noisome fumes from the snack bar
That repulsed anyone over eighteen.
Bruce won't sit on any more hoods
Right in the middle of the good parts.

Ten year old Davy would miss his profits
Selling his dad's Lucky Strikes to high schoolers.
Marilyn will have to think of someplace else
To do what she did best.

John Wayne, no longer confident
Behind the doors of the Alamo,
Was turned to vapor, coon hat and all
And projected to the dark beyond.

We just sat for awhile, thinking of things we'd seen.
Two or three titles came to mind
That stood above the action
That had surrounded us.

Richard D. Givens

CULTIVATING CULTURE

He mounts the green machine
Which chortles in a pall of black,
Rising as a curtain on the dawn mist.

Like Mario painting the Madonna,
There is an art to disking a field-
Straight, level, no mark of a wheel.

By the end of the row comes a favorite song.
"Strange Harmony" flows from the earphones;
The mouth under straw hat forms the words.

The returning run is overlapped, wheel-on-row.
The great vessel wallows upon a dirt sea-
Perhaps Tristan is sailing back to Cornwall.

Back and forth, East and West the goal may change
As the arias play to his ear.
Is it fickle Tosca or fatal Isolde that sings
"Mild and Softly He Is Smiling"?

Richard D. Givens

WHERE ARE THE FALCONS?

A crate falls from the loading dock
The sky grows ominously dark
A rush of wind amidst the applause of wings
A caldron of flapping shade erupts overhead
Dusting neighboring trees and utilities
With nervous, flying, swooping dots
To settle later, helicoptering, sticking
Like rain blown leaves up in the heights
Flying rats joust for space
In the arboreal, aerial alley
The sky rodents know no season
Always eating, flying, tapping, preening
Mating on the window sill, the steps
The lawn, the gutters, the eves
Always excreting, fighting, nesting
Raising young on the eves, the gutters
The lawn, the steps, the window sill
Always noisy, landing like parachute pigs
To break the attention of a dialog
Always nosey, peering into the pane
One eye, then the other, taking tiny notes
With a B-B brain
A slap on the shade sends the peepers upward
Outward into the nearby blue
Sparking primary and secondary stampedes
Again scattering atmospheric garbage
Excitement encouraging fresh dollops
On waxed paint, washed steps, new hats
Old statues, unsuspecting dogs
So much dinner on the wing
So much feathered falcon fodder

If all the flapping succumbed today
There would be more smell, more mites
More pigeons tomorrow
Oh, where are the falcons?

Richard D. Givens

PREFERENCES

Once upon a time in South Texas,
There was nothin' better than ridin' the wind
On dappled horses or motorbikes,
But the elements grow harsh with age.

Nothin's much changed in South Texas,
Except for stiff knees and weathered face,
Making the preferred conveyance
A climate-controlled pickup truck.

There's not too much to see in South Texas,
Except for maybe springtime, if it's rained
Before the wild flowers get to bloomin'...
...and then, it's mighty nice.

Now I digress, as most folks do in South Texas,
But it don't much matter what time I go
As long as the goin' is in my pickup.
It carries lots of gear, and very little company.

Don't much matter where I go in South Texas,
And it don't much matter that I'm not a farmer,
Rancher, roughneck or rodeo star.
Stars stick out too much...

...less'n you're one of thousands in South Texas,
Blending like the twinklers in a Texas night;
Just another cowboy wannabe in his pickup,
Glad to be ridin' in the wind.

Richard D. Givens

THE GATE KEEPER

North of somewhere, south of everywhere else,
The black morning lifts, revealing
Nature's nurture in the form of country fog
That left its mark in moisture on everything.

Four pickups congregate for work at the lease
And one is left to guard the main gate.
The cara cara glides upon the gray silence
Which is broken abruptly by coughing diesels
Of tractors and loaders in the back of the plot.
The gate man counts the dump trucks coming in-
Going out- mashing the caliche road to chalk.
The south wind today is the inhale
Of a storm from the north tomorrow.
Mesquite and prickly pears bordering the road
Have already donned their winter coats
Of beige dust, blown and fixed to the dew.

The boredom of gate watching, wheel counting
Is sequestered by a cacophonous "V" of sandhills
Honking away from the coming cold.
At Noon, the earth is quiet for an hour
And curious cud-chewers amble across the pasture
To peruse the phenomenon of stillness.
Too soon, the ten-wheelers are on the move-
Powdering the world once again.

Even the fire ants (those not crushed
By the onslaught of rubberized terror)
Can gain little purchase in their traverse
Through the pulverized surface of the entrance.

There are two visitors in the afternoon:
The compressor mechanic- lost- looking for a rig,
The old farmer- to complain about fast trucks and dust.
Sunshine appears at last, just before dusk
And slightly warms the hazy red air.

The pickup drivers wave as they pass,
Depositing one final layer of geologic ash.
The gate is swung shut and chained.
The guard climbs aboard the last conveyance
And thinks of home in an hour-and-a-half
And with eyes closed, composes lines for a poem.

Richard D. Givens

W-E, THE RIVER

Sabes dónde está la Nolana
I ask
Nolana *es la calle donde yo trabajaba,*
donde estaba la oficina

She says *yes*
She knows the direction of the office where I used to work
She positions her body in Sullivan City 40 miles away and
looks toward Nolana
That is North, I say.
Nolana is North
North and South are a pair,
and the river is always South.

Jake walks in
She wants me to stop talking
Jake has tried to teach her North and South
and she doesn't want him to know that she is trying to learn
with me
where East and West is to this North and South.

Jake catches the tension in the air
asks why I'm upset
I say it's not you
I'm trying to talk to my mother.

Jake exits
Do you know how to spell the word "we"?
Like *we go to the movies*
Like *we go to the store*
Like *we are dying mother*, but I don't say it

We
W-E

I point to the letters on the inside of the washer machine lid
The letters
W-E
Inside the cover of the washer the lid reads
*How to use your **Washer**:*
Read owner's guide and operating instructions
*for complete use and car**E** information.*

But my mother is no longer listening to me
Mom, the river is always South, I say
      but I feel the river in my toes
And look North towards Nolana
that is North, and as long as you know where North is
the river will always be behind you.

We
is in front, mom
W-E

The word spelled out as you look at
We
W-E
We are me and you, mother
trying to talk as you silence yourself in the shame of not
knowing.

We
are me and you, mother
West and East

This is where I begin,
where I remember the river
in the conversation I try to have with my mother
as she refuses to learn
she says
They think I am a *burra*

a donkey
another word for not smart,
but I will show them.

But she shuts out my words.
This is where I remember the river
in my mother's ears deaf to any learning
in my anger for her resistance
this is the river behind us
Behind me
Behind we
w-e
me and you mother
me and
u

Verónica Sandoval

MEXICO WHO

My mother echoes through the hallways of our home,
she shapes and reshapes stories that make her weep like a
12 year old girl.
My mother carries rivers in her chest,
rivers that she wishes to cross to find her way back to the
place before here.

My mother is a river,
and in her waters I found a place I call me,
Amerikana,
child of opportunity,
of Uncle Sam,
of a country that shapes and reshapes its story.

The Jazz in my heart
drowns in the voices from speaker machines,
conservative men with Godly ideas
drown out my song.

It's a song that sounds nothing like stars and stripes forever.
It's a song that needs the voices of *Los Panchos*.
It's a song that features Pedro Infante *a la ventana de una
            mujer bella,*
siempre enamorado.
It's a song that makes love to Jazz
while Jazz fondles the blues.
It's a song that
gives me
me

Amerikana,
an onion in the melting pot,
a child of the sun,
a summer blueberry girl.

If Bob Dylan could hear me now
with God on our side
we do things we would never think of,
we close up imaginary borders
and un-invite the tired masses,
ship them back on technicalities,
while slogan machines print out bumper stickers to place
the heads of our political party in positions of power.

This is all echoes,
it's political hoopla,
this is all techno with no ecstasy.

I remember a time when my president road on horseback
            with *Vicente Fox,*
now México has become *la sancha de Los Estados Unidos*

Mexico who
gave up its people like fruit, ripe, who built this country.
Mexico who
America invites and un-invites to its parties.
Mexico who
will not be kept out of me with concrete fences and barbed wire.
Mexico who
is my mother's eyes,
my father's nose,
my grandmother's breasts,
and the fire in my stomach.

Verónica Sandoval

NO, TROVADOR

No, Trovador
I will not let you sing to me about love
I will not be another conquest de guitar y amores de México
Yo no soy tu Amorcito Corazón
Tu muñeca de cuerda
I will not wait que salga la luna
I do not need your cositas bonitas
Quiero ser como Chavela Vargas
Quiero ser La Negra
Quiero nunca tener que engrasar las ejes de mi carreta
Quiero amar
a mi manera.

Verónica Sandoval

NEAR DWARAVATI, ON THE BEACH

He faces me in some glittering moonlit mindscape
—I almost feel the sea breeze and the still-warm sand—
His ageless eyes full of power that almost glows.

"Hello, Nara," he murmurs. "Here we always meet,
Near the water that was once milk. Do you know me?"

And for a moment I see it, the intaglio that is Krishna...
I become aware of my own filigree, trillions of silvery lines,
And I am Nara, that first mind in which danced
          the very first ideas,
Contemplating the god that arises in smoky traceries
From the newly created me.

"Friend of my mind..."
I begin, but the moment is gone,
          just an evanescent after-image
Fading like all the other fleeting apotheoses.

Yet I bend my focus inward,
Plunge into Brahman once again.

David Bowles

TRANS LUNBALKONO

Popoloj onde:
jarmilojn indiĝenoj,
    poste Hispanoj,
kurte ĉi Usonanoj. . .
Kiom da iroj, venoj!
    La tutan nokton
plaĝe la Golf' murmuris
    trans fenestro de
mia dormo. Voĉa surf'
en sablon forsusuris.

2005.01.12, Port-Isabel/Sud-Padre, Teksaso

Original Esperanto version.

Edwin de Kock

BEYOND A MOON BALCONY

People by waves:
for millennia natives,
afterwards Spaniards,
briefly these Americans. . .
Oh how they go, and come!
All night on the beach
the Gulf was murmuring
beyond a window
of my sleep. In the surf, into sand,
the voices rustled away.

Port Isabel/South Padre Island, 2005.01.12

English translation by the author.

Edwin de Kock

THIS IS WHERE I BELONG

Clandestine evenings
Peaceful serenity except for the voices of my kids,
The whisper of the wind, and the hymn of my home...
This is where I belong.

Where a raindrop splash is echoed through the walls of my ears,
And the inhale of earth tickles my nose with the scent of the wild.
Untamed and unruly flowers and grass grow in waterfalls
Not in imprisoned flower pots or caged fences.

Away from the powered evening lights of an illuminated city,
Where the only glistening you see,
Is the twinkling of the stars and brilliance of the moon
As it shines through the crevices of the night.

Rural landscapes where animals conversing are your alarm clock,
As well as the morning glow of the sun
       peering through your window
Not the honking of horns or escalating voices of traffic
Reminding you that another day has begun.

I am alive far away from the remnants of the city streets:
A distant soul in the calming embrace of the rural winds
That leave fingerprints on my skin and whisper into my ear...
This is where you belong.

Gwenda J. González

KARMA CUT ME CLEAN

Karma cut me clean
dreams come true as long as the sky's blue
same sentences, different words
i listen contently till every nerve gets bent
split and i swerve, curve my direction
what do you do when you fall in love
with your own reflection?
i'm neglecting thoughts
like they deserve what i bought them
send me clues and expect me to understand the news
i'm just a modern blues man, but damn i need a plan
and on this i stand, watch my house fan spin and spin

watch me lose and i never win
the few begin to study the trim
but again i'm in the ocean and i can't swim
few begin to study the trim
but again i'm in the ocean and i can't swim

look guys look what i did: i slipped and fell off a cliff
head-first like this time it was the worst
will next time be easier tease my fear of failure
tailor of rhymes creator of art perfectly thrown darts
off to another bad start tear me apart and call it a curse
i'll just rebuild it and make everything worse
i like to curse on this constant search
on this i stand watch my house fan spin and spin

i like to grin but i love to frown
it's like pain brings me up instead of down
just an artist in a town full ignorant clowns
i like to listen to waves and sounds they pave
the way to the ground, pound my temples
decide if it's complicated or simple

wrinkle the ironed rhymes solitary confinement
became my best friend and now we fight over time
let the light shine watch me climb to the top
just to fall every time laugh at me as i drop
arms flailing still just the student who's failing
i could swear someone's tailing me: i'm being followed
paranoia for ya and a bit of advice live life
like you don't get to do it twice, you get one chance
so dance and understand the stance

plans sink
falling off the brink of a well-defined sanity
society wants me to do this,
my family wants me to do that
i just sat in the back trying not to laugh
'cause this nation's situations are so incredibly racist
read between the lines and you'll realize this
bliss is fake and pain is anger's main man
i'm just the clam without a pearl: whirl me
in the wrong direction call my rhymes depression
i'll call it representing of constant correction
'cause if we don't fail, how will we move forward?
and stop chasing our tails with no reward
skin color became obsolete like phones with cords
yet still people fight and no longer with swords

they like to use guns
i like to use guitar chords and words that run
to fight my wars i said they no longer fight with swords
they like to use guns
i like to use guitar chords and words that run
just remember that you only get to live this one
i said just remember that you only get to live this one
so go take a walk and have some fun,
'cause this poem's done

Jonathan Corey Mangan

IN MY DREAMS

In my dreams I ask, what is color?
For here, there lives
No black. No white.
No raging racist river
To separate.
There survives only one color:
That of the human race.

In reality:
There exists
A black. A white.
The river WIDENS the canyon,
SEPERATING the races
So
FAR APART:
Black on one side.
White on the other.

In reality:
We suffer through the hatred,
Painful and almost too much to bear.
I watch
the ignorant burning stares melt the hearts of caring men.

And yet all too often
these compassionate ones,
Ignore what they see,
to continue with their day,
Only to become men who hide behind
The dark mask of
Racism.
Too weak to conquer their own fear of man.

To hide from reality,
I escape to my dreams.
My dreams, they tell me reality is worth the fight.
Always hoping and praying that one day in the world,
THE HUMAN RACE WILL PREVAIL.

I dwell in my dreams and sleep to fight my reality.

Kristin Michelle Keith

WHO'S NORM?

If **English** is the **Norm**... is **Spanish** the **worm**?
> **I too, have a dream that one day...**
Norm will stop wanting to kill our *Worm*.

If *English-Only*... does God understand *Spanish*?
> **I too, have a dream that one day...**
They'll see us as *permanent immigrants*
> instead of *recent immigrants*.

If I crossed the river... did I ever have a choice?
> **I too, have a dream that one day...**
They'll check *immigration status*
> and everything else we're carrying *within* us.

If *discrimination* is gone... why am I writing in English?
> **I too, have a dream that one day...**
We'll be free to speak or write in *Spanish*
> without killing *Norm*.

Are you Norm?

María Piedra

SPANISH AND ENGLISH

I think in Spanish
I speak in English

Sometimes it becomes Tex-Mex or Spanglish
Two languages in harmony

It is a border thing, Spanish and English
Where two cultures come together

Acculturation is inevitable
It is predictable

Where two cultures collide
The mixing of both languages

Turning English words into Spanish
Creating Tex-Mex and Spanglish

Living in the border of Texas and Mexico
is after all *magnífico!*

Ludivina V. Vásquez

THE OTHER SIDE

The sun sets;
The guns fire—
Shots are heard
Through the river's mire.

Children orphaned,
With nothing to eat;
Bodies lay lifeless
Upon the streets.

But here we stand,
On the other side,
Though the Border Wall
Can't shroud their cries.

María de la Luz Quiroga

SEARCHING RAINBOWS

People call me a lucky person,
but I prefer to see myself as successful,
for in everything I do I put my best effort,
and don't leave room for chance or venture.

If I had found without searching,
then you could call me special.
But if I have tirelessly sought and found,
then I deserve to say I triumphed.

Now, unfair would be to take all the credit for my thriving,
for I know I have been helped by Heaven.
But God hasn't sent down miracles like rain,
instead, He has inspired me by saying:
"I will back you up, no need to be afraid."

So with God as support and relentless work,
I will continue to accomplish my endeavors.
Because to find without searching I call luck,
but to search until finding, *that* I call *SUCCESS*.

Mónica G. Hernández

TAKE MY ADVICE

Inside me lies a burden,
of an unwanted friendship
with childish desires
for attention.
A worn out ear
no longer able to listen
to the hypocrisy
      selfishness
            the stories of how she became
               an adulteress.

"She's not good enough,"
      he says.
"You're controlling! A destroyer!
Leave my friend alone.
She's just got issues!"

Oh those issues,
never laid to rest.
But now I see
a falsehood of companionship.
I'm disgusted by your definition
of best friend.
      I'm sorry but I have to be honest.
      I think it's best that we don't stay friends.
Did I write my letter in invisible ink?

Uninvited guests are never welcomed.

Clarrissia Nerio

THE OTHER WOMAN

I know who she.
The Bitch,
The Demon,
The Home wrecker
The Whore.

Hiding behind every curtain,
                    Lurking.
Waiting for me to lose my temper,
Waiting for me to let her in.

I can't control her.

She yells at him
Makes him feel worthless
Makes him feel sad
Points out all his faults,

Smacks him
Spits on him
Throws things
Takes his money
Then leaves.

He always takes her back.

Like a toothache,
He's gotten used to her,
Doesn't notice the pain,
He expects it,
Learned to like it.

He makes love to her
With his pleas and cries,

Swears he'll never tell,
Promises no one will know.

But I know.

I can't get rid of her
He won't leave her,
He says he loves her,
Says she'll change.

But he never tells her to stay away.

I hate
Her I
Hate her
I want
Her
dead HE
Is MY
HUSBAND You are
Not YOU ARE
NOT welcome
HERE.

But she comes just the same.

He is torn between us,
One of us always waiting for him,
He never knows which.

Because sometimes I am me,
And sometimes,

I am the other woman.

Nina Medrano

FORGET ME NOT

Kiss me not, sir.

He kissed again.

Touch me not, sir.

He touched again.

Let me be, sir.

He remained.

Hurt me not, sir.

He left me pain.

Let me go, sir.

He held on tight.

NO SIR!

He locked the door.

Leave Me Be Sir.

We struggled to the floor.

I DO NOT WANT TO!

He did not care.

Leave that on, sir.

He left me bare.

GET OFF ME SIR!

DON'T

DON'T

PLEASE! I cried.

He did.
He did.
He did.
I died.

Kill me, sir.

He let me go.

Forget me not, sir,

For I will remember you so.

Nina Medrano

WHO IS SHE?

"She was a mother," said the artistic stretch marks
        painted on her belly.
"She was a single mother," said the dark circles
        that appeared every morning
        after calculating her monthly expenses.
"She was a hard worker," said her shoes
        scattered around her bed.
"She was beautiful," said her dresser
        filled with Mary Kay products.
"She never lost hope," said her bible,
        which she read every night.

Rosalia Arriaga

INVITACIÓN AL JALEO

Aún estoy por comenzar
y ya me encuentro perdida, sígueme
Nada ganas con quedarte allí en donde estas
Con tus sesos de queso y tus ojos de cera,
siempre en busca de alguien con quien te puedas relacionar.

Volaremos detrás de ciegos peces,
mirando de arriba a soldados de magnesio
Marchando con sus trajes de azul cielo,
frotando quedito vecinas raíces

Correremos detrás de los pájaros
Sobre lagos de pintura acrílica
Pintaremos bellísimos retratos
Con nuestros blancos pies sin zapatos

Los árboles mueven sus ramas
Para nunca a nuestra vista la luna bloquear
También consideran las estrellas
Y su fuerte vicio de cambiar color

Si nos da frío nos podemos cobijar
Con colchas de seda rellenas de magma
Y cuando nos desespere tanto calor
Podemos andar con solo la piel defendiendo nuestra alma

En ese mundo de infinita oportunidad
Anda el ganso de los llaveros
Desarmando todas las puertas,
las lleva sin orden en los cajones de su interior

Ni los fuertes ruidos, ni los fracasos
Allí no existe ni el pecado ni el mal
No habrá expectativas ni preocupaciones
No necesitaremos ni dinero ni pan

El espacio, solo el espacio,
Olvida el tiempo y su arma fatal
Un poco de seres locos
Y un mucho de nunca querer regresar

Dormiremos donde pertenecemos
Libres de horizontes
Donde nos pertenece todo y más
Libres de conclusiones

Yaresy Salinas

MADRE, SE TE QUEMÓ EL FIDEO

Mis zapatos rojos

Ahorcando mis dedos

Clara, muy clara

Y te quedas allí

Regresas y me escondo al verte venir

Te abrazo y te escucho

No me dejas morir

Metes fuerzas y cables

Un corte muy bello

El humo flotando

Fresas y perejil

Yaresy Salinas

BOHEMIA, AQUÍ SENTADA

Entre las evidencias de terror
En las paredes de mi castillo

Con la flauta de los niños aquí a mi lado
Con mis llaves, sin mis llaves, pinches llaves
Siempre se me pierden
Y la flauta dividiendo la duplicidad en mi cabeza

Y la gente la se fue
Y la Génesis también
Y yo aquí sentada
Con un DVD de chocolate rayado.
De aquel lado los actores se cambian
Y se pintan con más calma
Mientras yo me vuelvo loca
Con tantas largas pausas

El rojo, mi calor, el rojo
Y mí vestido allá guardado
En el asilo de plástico

Y recuerdo, yo recuerdo
Lo que tocan en el pasado
Lo bueno y mas lo malo
Pero lo bueno replicado
No sé si voy despacio
O si voy corriendo enseguida de la luz
Como el agua hirviendo
Que estaba a punto de congelar

Yaresy Salinas

VALS DEL DÍA NOCTURNO

Hoy por la noche
Dejaste a mi sol sin estrellas
Me quedé abrazada de nuestra calavera
En la primavera del verano

Canté risas sueltas
Con mariposas, sin sentimientos
Canté risas sueltas
Mil rencores, ningún despecho

Fui bailando lento al este
Pisando fuerte para marcar camino
Ya que estos estúpidos pies
Aun tienen la esperanza de que estés conmigo

Entre más me quemo más bailo, más floto, más vuelo
Y de repente se te pierde mi destino

Yaresy Salinas

VOLVER A NACER

Por poco y se me desprende mi alma
La muy caprichosa se negó a renunciar
Por fuera la peste de negro azufre
Adentro el olor de lavanda al brotar.

Esta alma arañaba destiladas venas
Con deseo de en ellas poderse atrapar
Se amarró con listones de plasma
Arrancados con su boca de oso polar.

"¡Sujétate dulce vapor juguetón!
La luna esta aferrada, contigo quiere bailar
Emborracho a la gravedad con sus blancos licores
Y por eso a mi cráneo viniste a dar."

Se difuso de ese obscuro rincón
De ese charco de nuevo se hizo mi mar
Salpicándole vida a mis telas de lino
Mi alma en silueta se volvió a formar.

Yaresy Salinas

BABY

Este pequeño rey
Me hace actuar curiosa
Brinco, grito
Soy su bufón

Esa carcajada libre
Me tiene derrumbando cielos
Nubes, estrellas
Lo que quiera el juguetón

Este bebe bonito
Me engrandece el corazón
Giro, canto
Su bufón, bufón

Esa carita hermosa
Me emite imaginación
Castillos, planetas
A donde quiera ir, yo voy

Este niño hermoso
Inicia danza en mis venas
Rio, gozo
Bufón, bufón, bufón

Yaresy Salinas

ABRAZOS Y NOCHES LIMITADAS

No me alcanza el día para brindarte mis amores
En el cubo de 16 horas no caben mis corazones
Le dedico una mueca al reloj
Por ser tan apresurado
Le aviento el dedo a la tierra
Por no girar más despacio

Me siento a tu lado
A contarte mis anécdotas
Tú duermes, yo hablo
En tus sueños mi historia se proyecta

Le robo a gente extraña momentos mal usados
A los que engañan, los que lloran
Y a los que se la pasan envidiando

Guardo esos momentos en un vacio frasco de café.
Por si los buscan, no tendrán olor que trazar
Suelto los momentos para ampliar
Los besos y abrazos que suelen no durar
Son esos momentos que me dejan respirar

Yaresy Salinas

ALUCINACIÓN DE ESPERANZA

Tengo esperanza de volverte a conocer
Esperaré aquí sentada
La belleza de tu amanecer

Creo tener esperanza de volver a escuchar tu aire
Déjame caer a tu lado y besar tu tibia carne

Perdí la esperanza en que nuestros caminos
Se volverán a topar
Nosotros vamos al frente
Y el tiempo hacia atrás

Yaresy Salinas

ACÚSTICA PERFECCIONADA

Conduzco mil sinfonías
Bajo esta pálida luz
Y mientras pétalos buscan el camino
Aquí sólo faltas tú

Conduzco mil sinfonías
En bocas propicias al mar
Pero a ti mi luna, mi sol
Nunca en exacto te podrán reflejar

Recojo ondas de acústica perfeccionada
Las adorno con alas de ángel civil
Les pinto un beso color oro
Y las mando derecho a tu ventana gris
Al llegar temprano velan tus sueños
Y a las siete en punto te recuerdan de mí

Conduzco mil sinfonías
En esta y cada noche sin fin
Con este anhelo que embriaga
Con esta esperanza que desgarra

Yaresy Salinas

RAYO ANGELICAL

Llegaste a mi vida como un rayo angelical.
Has sido la guía que me deja suspirar.
Cambiaste mi vida al paso real,
Me abriste los ojos y por eso, hoy,
Es este corazón el que te ofrezco yo.

No olvides nunca quién yo fui.
Toma el ejemplo para vivir
Con ese rayo angelical
Que inspira amor incondicional.
Tu sonrisa causa una emoción
Que no te puedo explicar.

Si con frecuencia te digo "te quiero",
Espero no sea un enfado más,
Sino un recuerdo de lo que te puedo dar.
Tal vez no sea mucho para ti, aún eres pequeña
Y no te darás cuenta de lo que me haces sentir.

Cambia tu vida al paso real,
Abre los ojos y ofrece ese corazón
Que solo así entenderás el amor que una madre da.
Toma el ejemplo para vivir con ese rayo angelical
Que inspira un amor incondicional.
No pierdas nunca ese rayo angelical.

Anna Lilia Castillo

AL CEMENTERIO DI LA VUELTA HOY

Al cementerio di la vuelta hoy.
Fui a darte una explicación,
¿Cómo es que sigo adelante yo?
Aún mi vida no tiene conclusión.
La vida me espera ya.
Hoy las flores pierden su fervor
Y la lluvia su claridad.
Viviste la vida hasta su fin.

Dame tiempo de decir adiós
A los pasos que juntos dimos.
Hoy las flores pierden su fervor
Y la lluvia su claridad.
Hay pureza en ese cielo azul.

Te das cuenta que esta soledad
Yo la tengo que reemplazar
Con aquel que hoy será la voz de mi eternidad.
Al cementerio di la vuelta hoy. No para despedirme,
Sino para decirte que mi vida busca conclusión.
Viviste la tuya hasta el final.

Al cementerio di la vuelta hoy.
Fui a darte una explicación,
Ya no hay tiempo que esperar.
Hoy doy un paso más para seguir adelante yo.

Anna Lilia Castillo

ESE CUARTO

Allí reímos como niños con placer de vivir juntos
Los momentos que con otros no pudimos compartir.
Ese cuarto blanco repugna un ardiente morado
Y su suelo rojo refleja el centro de nuestra intimidad.

Allí hay colores tan amor-atados como tu corazón
Que guarda esos golpes que suenan en mi interior.
A ese cuarto tan brillante, no me atrevo a escapar;
Guarda rasgos de ilusiones y sueños sin realizar.

Al otro lado de esa puerta se parecen presentar
Esas rosas que un día me pudiste regalar.
Ellas guardan los silencios
Que sólo tú y yo sabemos descifrar.

Aunque el cuarto sea blanco repugna de ese ardor.
Hay colores tan estropeados como tu corazón
Que guarda esos golpes que suenan en mi interior.
A ese cuarto tan brillante, no me atrevo a escapar;
Guarda rasgos de ilusiones y sueños sin realizar.

Anna Lilia Castillo

EL RÍO

El río es muerte
Como una tumba profunda
Devorando las almas sin piedad
Los cuerpos que flotan como troncos sin rumbo
Sus secretos como la corriente tan fuerte.

Gloría M. Alvarado

¿TENEMOS?

En el aire está el poder,
sembrado en la materia sin retorno,
de la oscuridad a la aniquiliación,

más allá del recuerdo
surge el espasmo de la fecundación,
la sorpresa de la memoria
cae al atardecer.

Venas de transición,
me vomito y me creo a mí mismo,
automatismo de la concepción,

actores esporádicos, momentáneos,
luz futura del huevo que contiene
el embrión olvidadizo,
creatura del hoyo negro,
con tan sólo una mueca,
un leve movimiento,
un circulo comienza
y nunca se termina de completar.

Edwin Sandoval

CONTRIBUTOR BIOGRAPHIES

Álvaro Rodríguez

Álvaro Rodríguez has been writing since childhood and, in fact, did his best work when he was 11. With filmmaker Robert Rodriguez, he is the co-writer of the wishing-rock children's movie SHORTS (2009), and MACHETE (2010) starring Danny Trejo and Robert DeNiro, and is the screenwriter of the vampire western FROM DUSK TILL DAWN: THE HANGMAN'S DAUGHTER (2000). His short stories (including a *Pushcart Prize* nominee) have appeared in *The Mesquite Review*, *flashquake*, *BorderSenses* and *Popcorn Fiction*.

David Bowles

David Bowles was born in 1970 in Upper Marlboro, Maryland, but has lived the majority of his life in South Carolina and the Río Grande Valley of south Texas, where he presently resides with his wife and children. Since 1994 he has worked in public education, as a teacher, administrator and university professor. A writer of young adult fiction, Latino-themed magical realism and politically speculative science fiction, Bowles has launched his *D'Angelo Chronicles* through VAO Publishing, a division of Valley Artistic Outreach. In April of 2011, Absey & Co. published *The Seed: Stories from the River's Edge*, a collection of YA short stories the author collaborated with his wife, Angélica Maldonado, to create.

Angélica Maldonado

Originally from Monterrey, Nuevo León, Angélica is the executive director of Valley Artistic Outreach. She teaches recycled art and promotes local artists when she is not working on her own upcycled furniture projects. In April of 2011, Absey & Co. published *The Seed: Stories from the River's Edge*, a collection of YA short stories she collaborated on with David Bowles.

Yaresy Salinas

Yary Salinas is a Hispanic female poet from Mission, Texas. She has participated in various poetry events such as "Letras en el estuario" and "Los santos días de la poesía." Her fresh, mischievous poetry is mainly influenced by passion, music, and science. It is saturated with surreal images, unexpected juxtapositions, and brazen metaphors.

María Ramírez

María Paula Ramírez is originally from Donna, Texas. She has been a teacher, principal and central office administrator in the public schools and correctional settings. Paula has had short stories published by International Publications and Red Rock Press and has self-published a collection of childhood stories. Mrs. Ramírez and her husband presently live in New Braunfels, Texas.

Daniel Tyx

Daniel Tyx teaches English at South Texas College in McAllen, where he lives with his wife, son, two dogs and a cat. "First Day" is a chapter from a novel-in-progress titled *The Sir*.

Félix Omar Vela

Félix Omar Vela describes himself thus: "Educator, philosopher; here to make a difference in the lives of the people who happen to stumble across mine. Knowledge is endless—learn as much as possible whenever possible."

Evangelina Ayon

Evangelina Ayon was born near the pacific coast in central Mexico before moving to the Rio Grande Valley as a child. She learned to speak English in school and quickly became immersed in books and storytelling. Currently a senior at the University of Texas Pan-American, she looks forward to continuing writing after graduation.

Lois Marie Garza

Lois Marie Garza was a businesswoman, mother and storyteller in the Río Grande Valley for many years. Her present contribution is being published posthumously by her family.

Charlene Bowles

Charlene is a student and artist whose work has been most recently published in the middle-grades title *Swift the Cat-Human, Book 1: Mix-Up*, for which she designed the cover and did interior illustrations.

Robert Brown

Robert Brown attributes his love of writing to his fourth grade teacher, Hugo Soto, who inspired him to embrace his macabre style of storytelling at an early age. Robert, who lives in McAllen, Texas, is an aspiring novelist and screen writer.

Cindy Jáimez

Cindy is a seventeen-year-old junior at Business, Education, and Technology Academy (B.E.T.A.) at Edinburg, TX. She is involved at her school with several extracurricular activities and enjoys being part of them. She also volunteers in her community during the weekends and in her free time, she enjoys reading and writing.

Virgilio B. Valencia

Virgilio graduated from the University of the Philippines with a Bachelor's degree in Education, major in English. He has extensive experience in education and training, having taught high school students in a Jesuit school and trained health professionals at the World Health Organization Regional office in Manila, the Philippines. He lists painting, running, and sleeping as his hobbies.

Alfredo Ortiz

Alfredo Ortiz is a modest student. He enjoys listening to music, which is how he spends most of the day. Alfredo plans on becoming an RN to help others. You can typically find Alfredo with headphones on and iPod in hand, listening to music. He's a quiet guy, but gains confidence when a good friendship is established. Overall, he's a good friend to have.

Javier David González

Javier David González is a passionate writer, poet and avid lyricist. Initially inspired by writing lyrics, he evolved into writing short stories and dialogues. Having completed his first published work, "Child Number Five," which depicts childhood isolation, he is now finishing a children's' short story dealing with the innocence of childhood love.

Matthew Madrigal

Matthew Madrigal is a student at Texas A&M University - College Station. He is currently majoring in history with a minor in English. He loves to search for knowledge in every dark corner he seems to find. He thoroughly enjoys reading dust-accumulated literature, highly acclaimed essays and short stories, writing in every sense of the word, and taking long thoughtful walks along the beach.

Olga Lidia Cervantes

Olga Lidia Cervantes was born in Tamaulipas, Mexico and at the age of 10 she migrated to the U.S. She is married and has four adorable children. Olga Lidia obtained her bachelor's degree from the University of Texas-Pan American in May 2005 and recently received her Master's Degree in May of 2010. She enjoys writing poems and short stories about her memorable childhood.

Richard D. Givens

Richard D. Givens started writing poetry at age sixteen. He graduated from Mercedes High School and earned a B.A. degree in English and Mass Communication from U.T. Pan Am. He received the Young Poet Award in 1972 from the R.G.V. Chapter of the Poetry Society of Texas and self-published a small volume of satirical and humor poems in 1975, *I Wish the World Could Die with Me*. His works also appeared in the *Pan-O-Rama* and *Winter's Half*, anthologies. Givens was a member of the Valley Poets Workshop for over 25 years, and during that time had works published in the anthologies *Bluesonnets* and *Butterfly Collection*. Named Honorary Bard by the Scottish Society of South Texas, he was published in *Dubh Ghlase*, the Clan Douglas periodical. Two poems were in the first edition of the *Mesquite Review* in 1997, followed by a short story, later that year. A poem was also selected for *Riversedge* (UT Pan American

Press) the same year. He was a 3rd Prize recipient for the West Virginia Poetry Society contest of 1998 and had an Honorable Mention for the Joseph V. Hickey Memorial Award that year. Givens works in oilfield sales and lives with his wife Karen and son Trevor in McAllen.

Verónica Sandoval

Verónica, also known as "Lady Mariposa," is an old-school chola, street poet, spokenword artist. Her writing has appeared in publications such as *Gallery*, *BorderSenses*, *Lung* and El Tecolote Press. She has a spoken word album entitled *Hecha en El Valle: Spoken Word & Borderland Beats* with Keytar Dreamz and ChulaRecords.

Edwin de Kock

Edwin de Kock (1930-), a polyglot immigrant, is a famous Esperanto poet with ten volumes of original poetry to his credit. His *Sub fremdaj ĉieloj* (*Under Foreign Skies*), 2007, contains several poems with Hispanic and related themes. He has also published in English and Afrikaans. One of his other passions is the study of history and prophecy. In this genre, his latest work, *The Truth About 666,* comprises more than 850 pages. It appeared as a digital publication in 2011. De Kock was a professional educator for more than thirty-five years in South Africa, Korea, and the United States. He finished this career by teaching writing at the University of Texas, Pan American, Edinburg, from 1996 to 2000.

Gwenda J. González

Gwenda says of herself, "My name is Gwenda Jean Gonzalez and I have been a teacher for ten years at Captain D. Salinas II Elementary in Donna, TX. I am the mother of three wonderful children whom have often been the inspiration for many of my writings. What began as an escape at the age of twelve has turned into a passion, and I enjoy creating a canvas filled with words. As a fourth grade teacher I have the privilege to teach the art of writing to my students as they embark on their own mural of words through written expression."

Jonathan Corey Mangan

Spoken-word/lyricist Jonathan Corey Mangan was born in Weslaco, in 1990 and grew up in McAllen. His immediate family includes: a fly scientist from Virginia, a fish artist from California and a budding physicist/mathematician who lives in Boston. He is the author of *Coreyology*, a collection of 53 poems celebrating the transitive powers of the creative process and his personal journey through and independent triumph over depression and addiction, published and available at Smashwords.com. Those interested in performances or collaborations may contact him at abcoreydefgh@hotmail.com.

Kristin Michelle Keith

Kristin says of herself, "A 2003 graduate of the University of Kentucky, I moved to the Rio Grande Valley in 2008. It was at this time that I changed careers and entered the education field through course work with ACT of the RGV. God blessed me with a wonderful opportunity when he provided me with a classroom at P.S. Garza Elementary, in Donna, Texas, where I am currently in my third year of teaching. In my free time I enjoy reading a good book, spending time with my friends and family, and working with the elementary-aged kids and teens at my church."

María Piedra

María says of herself, "I was born in Nuevo Progreso, Tamaulipas, Mexico (otherwise known as *Las Flores*). I came to the USA when I was 17 years old. I love to read, write, sing and talk. I am a creative elementary teacher who is NOT *'Waiting for Superman'* but *becoming Superman* regardless of school politics. I believe in teaching with love. I have God as the author of my life, and I believe in him because nobody has given or offered more than what He has. Writing has giving me the opportunity to collaborate and be the coauthor of life. I am inspired by authors... need a coauthor?"

Ludivina V. Vásquez

Ludivina V. Vásquez was born on July 26, 1970 in McAllen, Texas and raised in a small farm in Donna. She is the daughter of Mexican immigrants and the fifth of nine siblings. She attended the University of Texas-Pan American and double majored in Spanish and English receiving a bachelor's degree in December 2008. She reached her dream of becoming a teacher with the support of her family, parents, brothers and sisters. For the past ten years, she has dedicated her life to working with non-profit agencies with the mission to strengthen Valley disadvantaged families through educational programs.

María de la Luz Quiroga

María de la Luz Quiroga is a 16-year-old junior at Donna High School. Her hobbies include reading, writing, and drawing (she is mainly known for her Etch-A-Sketch art). She is a Río Grande Valley native, currently living with her parents, brother and sister. This is her first publication.

Mónica G. Hernández

Mónica G. Hernández was born in Victoria, México, on January 27, 1979. She holds an Accounting degree from Tecnológico de Monterrey and a MBA from UTB. She enjoyed working in her field area, but decided to switch to a career where she would be more in contact with children and have the opportunity to help those in need. She then became an elementary bilingual teacher in Donna ISD, and is currently pursuing an MA in Bilingual Education to better understand the needs of her students. Such transition to a new career and country has been—and continues to be—full of challenges.

Clarrissia Nerio

Clarrissia says of herself, "I feel, I write, I create. Somewhere between the disciplinarian and the rebel lie chaos and a bit of poetry."

Nina Medrano

Nina Marie (Bone) Medrano was born and raised in Barryton, Michigan. In 2002, she came on vacation to Mission Texas to visit some friends of her family. She enjoyed her stay there so much that she did not return to Michigan until 2005 and that was only to retrieve her belongings. Since then she has made the Río Grande Valley her home and adds her voice to the chorus when people say, "I wasn't born here, but I got here as quick as I could."

Rosalia Arriaga

Rosalia Arriaga says of herself, "I am the youngest of ten children. I was raised in the humble city of Donna, Tx. by a single mom, Celia Almanza, who persevered until she saw her daughter have a career. My mother taught me to be hardworking and to never lose hope!

Anna Lilia Castillo

Anna Lilia Castillo is a lifelong native of the Río Grande Valley. Anna Lilia attended the University of Texas Pan American and is currently working for Donna ISD as a Middle School Teacher. Her hobby is writing short poems for her personal collection. The crisis on the border has rendered her mute on the subject since relatives dearest to her heart live there. She is considering placing those emotions on paper in the near future.

Gloria M. Alvarado

Gloria says of herself, "I was born and raised in Alamo, TX. The third child out of six children born to Pascual and Enedina Longoria Moreno. I graduated from Pharr-San Juan-Alamo in 1975 and graduated from Pan American University in 1980. I worked for PSJA ISD from 1980 until 2001 as a special education classroom teacher and special education supervisor. In 1986 I obtained my Master's degree from Texas A & I Kingsville, Texas. I taught for the Texas Youth Commission from 2002 until 2004. In 2004 I started several businesses: East Crockett Apartments, LAHS Adult Day Care Center and two childcare centers in McAllen. In 2008 I began to teach for Donna ISD. I have been married to Celso Alvarado Jr. for thirty-five years and we have two married sons, Celso Pablo (Mari) and Erik Gabriel (Connie). I have a grandson, Matthew Illidan, and one granddaughter, Summer, due in July."

Edwin Sandoval

Edwin Sandoval was born in Monterrey, Mexico in 1982. He has lived in Texas since the age of 16 and became a naturalized U.S. citizen in the year 2004. Since childhood he has been interested in different artforms like drawing and sculpting. He began practicing drawing and clay/plasticine sculpting supported by his mother, who recognized an early enthusiasm for creative childhood play. Later in his pre-teen times, he experimented with some writing but never continue practicing. During his adolescent years he turned to painting and comic book styles of drawing. At the age of 18 and later on, he formed different punk rock bands in Mexico, which became famous on the underground circuit for their lyrics and onstage performances. Both the lyrics and performances ideas were constructed by the self- taught artist, who became more and more familiar with poetry and song writing. He drew, wrote and published an audio comic book for his last band that became a great seller during the band's shows. He is now focusing in different artforms at the same time, especially mixing drawing with poetry, and creating an artform which will enable the audience to know the language of mystery through art.

Made in the USA
Las Vegas, NV
18 March 2023